WILDE

INTRODUCTION BY STEPHEN FRY

SCREENPLAY AND AFTERWORD BY
JULIAN MITCHELL

DOVE
BOOKS

A Samuelson Production
A Brian Gilbert Film

Stephen Fry Jude Law Vanessa Redgrave Jennifer Ehle

Gemma Jones Judy Parfitt Michael Sheen

Zoë Wanamaker Tom Wilkinson

Casting Director Sarah Bird
Editor Michael Bradsell
Production Designer Maria Djurkovic
Costume Designer Nic Ede
Director of Photography Martin Fuhrer
Sound Recordist Jim Greenhorn
Line Producer Nick O'Hagan
Music Composed and Conducted by Debbie Wiseman

Executive Producers
Michiyo Yoshizaki
Michael Viner
Deborah Raffin
Alex Graham
Alan Howden

Original screenplay by Julian Mitchell
from *Oscar Wilde* by Richard Ellmann

Producers
Marc Samuelson
Peter Samuelson

Director Brian Gilbert

Screenplay developed with the assistance of British Screen Finance Ltd, London, England and the support of the European Script Fund, an initiative of the MEDIA Programme of the Commission of the European Communities.

For Dove International Inc: Michael Viner, Deborah Raffin, Mary Aarons.

For Samuelson Entertainment Ltd: Rachel Cuperman, Ian Thomson.

Grateful thanks to Merlin Holland, Lucy Ellmann, Alexander Walker, John Wagstaff, Sally Griffiths, Michiyo Yoshizaki, Reinhard Brundig, Alex Graham, Alan Howden, Peter Smith, David Elstein, Jane Barclay, Sharon Harel, Anthony Jones, Premila Hoon, Lisbeth Savill, Simon Perry.

www.oscarwilde.com

ONTENTS

There Never Was Such a Man

STEPHEN FRY

In today's cinema, if you are British, voiced like an old wireless set, approaching forty at dangerous speed, well over six feet in height, amply padded to the point of minor obesity and endowed with a complexion not unlike that of freshly applied window putty, there are few leading roles for which you are suited. Drug barons, emotionally constipated colonial husbands about to be left for floppy-haired darlings, Gestapo interrogators, prosecuting attorneys, corrupt asset-strippers, pederastic bishops, callous staff officers, sadistic prison governors and lilac-haired megalomaniacs with Persian cats on their laps — these are your future. It would be footling and moronic to complain. A lifetime of such roles would not be something to look back on with displeasure. The devil usually gets the best tunes after all and age, raddling and increased weight are no drawback. If any film actor is to be pitied it is the leading man or woman who doesn't ripen into a Sean Connery or a Shirley Maclaine. Their time in the sun will be short.

However.

As someone for whom the opening description could have been written (and, by one of those weird coincidences that make you shiver and go all gooey, it was), I always felt a small, secret longing to try, just once, something a little more taxing, a little more terrifying, a little less obvious. Long resigned to the fact that I could never play Hamlet or Bond, I have nonetheless felt that it was pretty pointless to spend all one's life in the shallow end of Drama's swimming-pool. It's safer there and easier to climb out, of course, but every now and then one can't help looking up with a twinge of envy at the big boys bouncing on the high board and diving in so gracefully. Even if I belly-flopped and came up choking to embarrassed silence from the gallery I could go to my grave knowing that I had tried.

For many years I have known that Oscar Wilde was one of the few major parts I might be lucky enough to be offered. I knew this not because I believed in it myself, but because I had been told it. I had been told since I was quite young and was told it with gathering frequency as my girth thickened and the flesh on my face began to record every plate of pasta and every glass of vodka and tonic that had been pushed through it. 'Has anyone ever told you you look just like Oscar Wilde?' is one of those questions like, 'What's Rowan Atkinson like, then?' or, 'I say, Jeeves, what have you done with Bertie?' that I have got very used to hearing over the past ten years.

Some time ago, I was in a film directed by Kenneth Branagh called *Peter's Friends*. Although the part I played was that of Peter, you couldn't call it the title role, because that went, if you want to be ridiculously pedantic, and I always do, to the Friends. Kenneth Branagh and I talked during the filming about the possibility of doing something about Oscar Wilde. I had received a very charming letter from Lucy Ellmann, daughter of Richard Ellmann, author of the huge and revealing biography of Wilde that had recently come out and which was subsequently used by Julian Mitchell as the basis of much of the screenplay you are about to read. Lucy Ellmann said in this letter that she imagined me as the very person to play Oscar Wilde and wondered if I had any plans to do so.

At the time I was living in the Savoy Hotel.

I love that sentence. I love it so much that I was sorely tempted to begin this whole Introduction with it and work backwards from there.

At the time I was living in the Savoy Hotel.

I'm so sorry. I just had to write it again. We shall return to the Savoy later for it features more than a little in my life and in Oscar's.

(I should note here that I am going to refer to Oscar Fingal O'Flahertie Wills Wilde as Oscar throughout. It is very difficult and wasteful of ink to keep calling him Oscar Wilde, and while calling him Oscar may seem over-familiar, as if one was claiming to have known him or to have been part of his circle, to call him Wilde somehow seems to me to be worse. It suggests the tone of those dark Victorian nasties in Dundreary weepers and black frock-coats who would call him 'that man, Wilde' and hiss about 'the Wildean vice' through clenched teeth. There are those, after all, who combine an unusual enough given name and/or a great enough reputation to have transcended surnames and to live in the public realm simply as Leonardo or Michelangelo or Groucho or Jesus. Oscar Wilde is such another. There is, ultimately, only one Oscar. I hope the Hammerstein, Levant, Peterson and de la Renta families won't be too affronted by this claim.)

The reasons for me living in the Savoy Hotel are complicated and actually more to do with Noël (Coward, not Edmunds) than Oscar, but nonetheless the fact remains that while I was filming *Peter's Friends* I was living in the Savoy Hotel. I mention this not just because I like the sentence . . .

At the time I was living in the Savoy Hotel.

. . . although that should be reason enough, but because, while not a superstitious man, I am also very far from being substitious, if there is such a word (and there isn't). Like most people I respond to chimes, resonances, coincidence, synchronicity, serendipity, and that mother jazz. While I would walk a long way to be offered the chance to slap a businessman who employed a shaman or an astrologer (I believe such an attitude is described in the shamanic trade, sham for short, as 'negativity') I would also cheerfully allow an adventitious coincidence or a happy accident to confirm a decision.

The collaboration with Kenneth Branagh over an Oscar film never got off the ground. A few letters flew back and forth between self and Lucy Ellmann, a promising first draft was written by Kim Harris and sporadic talk continued while Kenneth Branagh went off and shot seventeen or so major feature films elsewhere around the world. In the meantime, I was asked to play Oscar in an American TV western series called *Ned Blessing*. It was a small cameo, more of a ring than a brooch. Set during Oscar's tour of the USA, he helps out the hero's love life and rides in a fringed buggy. It wasn't an insult to Oscar, however: it showed a knowledge of his kindness and physical strength and did nothing to perpetuate the idea prevalent in some people's heads that he was a mimsy, brittle sort of creature with crimped hair, an enormous buttonhole and a smart line in self-satisfied repartee. It was also directed by David Hemmings, working with whom was such a pleasure in itself that the project would have been worth doing even if the whole thing were ill-founded and absurd.

Years before even this event I had enjoyed meetings at the old Zanzibar Club in London with Anwar Bhatti and Marcel Berlins (the legal journalist who sets the *Guardian* newspaper's fiendish Saturday quiz and looks bizarrely like Albert Einstein) about a possible film of Oscar Wilde in America – following his lecture tour from East to West.

While working on a film called *I.Q.* in Princeton, New Jersey (starring Walter Matthau as Albert Einstein and looking bizarrely like Marcel Berlins) I happened across a script about Oscar's life called *Feasting with Panthers* by David Hare.

It was as if Dame Nature were gathering up her skirts and preparing for a final assault. Oscariness was everywhere. We were approaching a whole slew of centennial markers, a hundred years since the first night of *The Importance of Being Earnest*, a hundred years since the first of the three terrible trials.

Also around this time I met Merlin Holland, Oscar's grandson by Vyvyan Holland, second of Oscar's two beloved sons. Merlin seemed actively to encourage the idea of me one day playing his grandfather and we talked about Oscar and how a film could record the circumstances of that extraordinary life while conveying the nature of the man, his astounding intellect, his art, his work, his deep love for his family. Merlin, I should say, is not a professional grandson, not pompously the Keeper of the Sacred Flame. After all, like every human being, he has four grandparents. He is as much the grandson of Oscar's wife Constance and of his mother's parents as he is 'Grandson of Oscar'. Nonetheless, the work of his father in collecting

Oscariana and assembling an active scholastic and family archive is something he keeps alive with great commitment and knowledge.

There are few writers around whom a greater literature has grown up than Oscar Wilde. There have been many biographies of Oscar himself, and biographies of his mother, his friends and all the members of his 'circle', from Lord Alfred Douglas to Reggie Turner. Only yesterday, for example, I received in the same post bound proofs of two different books from two different publishers, one called *Wilde's Last Stand: Decadence, Conspiracy and the First World War* and the other *André and Oscar: Gide, Wilde and the Gay Art of Living.* I should imagine Merlin gets a postbag like this everyday of the week. Not just bound proofs, either: letters from authors, academics, dramatists, film producers or documentary makers proposing some new work and often seeking the advice, approval or imprimatur of Oscar's grandson. Merlin makes a great and noble effort not to go out of his way to endorse any one project. Nonetheless, to have met him and feel that he did not regard my interest in or thoughts about Oscar as ignorant or impertinent was very important to me.

A few months later he invited me to contribute a subscription to the installation of a memorial window to Oscar in Westminster Abbey. In February 1995, at a remarkable service, this window was consecrated. A hundred years earlier *The Importance* and the Marquess of Queensberry's infamous open card had been about to burst upon the world and register Victorian theatre's open high water mark and Victorian society's scumline. Seamus Heaney made a magnificent eulogy and, as the service ended, Merlin's mother, Oscar's daughter-in-law, walked arm-in-arm with the Marchioness of Queensberry down the Abbey, a rapprochement that brought tears to the eyes of the carved monarchs in their tombs on either side of the aisle.

Five days later I fled a London theatre and created a minor, wholly banal and insignificant scandal of my own.

We cut discreetly to more or less the same

time the following year. I am in the bar of the Savoy hotel to talk to a film producer called Marc Samuelson and a director called Brian Gilbert. They have sent me a screenplay by Julian Mitchell. We are gathered to talk about it.

I have read the screenplay and I love it. I loved the movie that the Samuelsons and Gilbert made of *Tom and Viv*. I love the fact that they have chosen to meet me here in the Savoy – contrary to popular belief, such a rendezvous is not usual, film people do not spend their lives in five star hotels. They have chosen it because it is a Wildean place. I love too their honesty and their attitude. They tell me that they think they like the idea of me playing Oscar but they are worried about raising the money for the film on the basis of my name, which is far from huge in cinema box office terms. I tell them that I understand completely. I also understand that, after the embarrassments of the previous year, I can quite see that I am something of an insurance risk. I tell them I am very prepared to do a screen test, and that I am happy to be chained up at nights under the eye of a Rottweiler to stop me from wandering off to Belgium.

Inside, however, I know. I am resigned. Films require film stars. I leave the Savoy feeling that it is unlikely that I shall play Oscar in their film but that at least I will enjoy watching it when it comes out. I cast a look back at the hotel where once I lived for a short time and where Oscar spent so many weeks sharing a room with Bosie. Savoy staff were called as witnesses in court to testify to, amongst other things, stained bed sheets in Oscar's suite. The theatre here gave its name to the Savoy Operas of Gilbert and Sullivan. It was their operetta *Patience*, making fun of Oscar and the aesthetic movement, that caused the producer Richard D'Oyly Carte to send Oscar on his tour of the United States so that Broadway audiences might understand the nature of the type of man *Patience* was guying. All those little connections gather in my head and I sigh at What Might Have Been.

The next day my agent calls me to tell me that the Samuelsons and Gilbert do want me for Oscar, that they have decided to try and raise money without a big name for the lead. I meet Jude Law in Marc Samuelson's house and there is no question that he would be perfect for Lord Alfred Douglas. He is only twenty-three but knows more about films than most people twice his age. Vanessa Redgrave has agreed to play Speranza, Wilde's mother. I sacrifice a young aubergine and spread its entrails on the altar. The auguries are excellent. The script improves with every pass Julian and Brian Gilbert make through it. I remain calm, however. There is, as they don't say in cricket, many a slip twixt wicket keep and gully (that's a meaningless joke for American readers, but let me assure you that it is nonetheless of the very highest quality). Marc and Peter Samuelson still have to raise the money and this is not easy. A film of Christopher Hampton's *Total Eclipse* has not done well in America. It stars Leonardo di Caprio and David Thewlis, a better star name pedigree than *Wilde*

will boast. It centres around the sexual and literary relationship between the French poets Rimbaud and Verlaine. Although this might be considered to be completely irrelevant to our project, in the minds of many American distributors it could set up one of those *idées fixe* for which Hollywood is justly celebrated: literary faggots = box office poison.

The brothers Samuelson have the tenacity of a kennel of Jack Russells, however, and after a three-volume novel of false starts, near misses, night sweats and the whole carnival of terrors which are the absolute norm in British film pre-production the cameras begin to roll.

I write this before the film has entered that state known as the fine cut. What the world will make of it, or will have made of it by the time you read this, I cannot tell. No one ever can. It is William Goldman's rule of film making and holds as true today and in Britain as it did in America twenty years ago when Goldman wrote *Adventures in the Screen Trade*. NO ONE KNOWS ANYTHING. I have had my time in the deep end and, thanks to a cast and crew of remarkable talent and equally remarkable kindness and sympathy, I have enjoyed the process of making the film so much that I feel I can return to perverted bishops and epicene villains with a glad heart.

One thing I do know, however, and that the Samuelsons, Gilbert and Mitchell and all of us set out to do our best by Oscar: not to glamorize, not to sensationalize, not to vulgarize. If the film does not show Oscar in *all* his glory, that is because a hundred and fifteen minutes of film could never do that to anyone's life, let alone to a life as rich and strange as Oscar's. To *show* his life in a film is not the same as to *tell* his life in a book. You cannot show an author, intellectual and artist like Wilde working as you might be able to show a painter painting or dancer dancing.

Oscar himself said that he put his talent into his work and his genius into his life. I hope you enjoy Julian Mitchell's script of that life and that, if you enjoyed the film too, it will turn you straight to the works of Oscar Wilde. There never was such a man.

I can best end with the words Richard Ellmann uses to complete his biography:

> *He belongs to our world more than to Victoria's. Now, beyond the reach of scandal, his best writings validated by time, he comes before us still, a towering figure, laughing and weeping, with parables and paradoxes, so generous, so amusing, and so right.*[1]

STEPHEN FRY

[1] Richard Ellmann, *Oscar Wilde*, Penguin Books, 1988.

CAST PORTRAITS

Oscar Wilde
Stephen Fry

Lord Alfred Douglas
Jude Law

Constance Wilde
Jennifer Ehle

Ada Leverson
Zoë Wanamaker

Lady 'Speranza' Wilde
Vanessa Redgrave

The Marquess of Queensberry
Tom Wilkinson

Robert Ross
Michael Sheen

John Gray
Ioan Gruffudd

Edward Carson
David Westhead

Cyril and Vyvyan Wilde
Jack Knight and Laurence Owen

FROM LEFT TO RIGHT: *Charles Parker* (Mark Letheren),
Alfred Wood (Benedict Sandiford), *Alfred Taylor*
(Michael Fitzgerald), *Oscar Wilde* (Stephen Fry),
Lord Alfred Douglas (Jude Law) and *Rent boy* (Sasha Bennett).

Lady Mount-Temple Judy Parfitt

Charles Gill
Peter Barkworth

ABBREVIATIONS

Cont.	continued
O/S	offstage
POV	point of view
V/O	voice over

The Screenplay by Julian Mitchell

1

EXTERIOR

Leadville, Colorado

1882. DAY

*Clouds of dust are rising as PEOPLE gallop up on horses. There is great excitement –
someone is coming – 'Where is he? Where is he?' – then a shout – 'Here he is!'*

*A large group of MINERS old and young are gathered at the head of the pit workings. A
great vista of mountains stretches to either side. Old mining shacks, a weighing shed and
sluicing creek are near. Most of the MINERS wear revolvers.*

*Accompanied by a welcoming party OSCAR WILDE, sitting atop a mule, is being led
towards the mine, head and shoulders above the throng. He is not quite thirty, dressed in a long
green coat with fur collar and cuffs and a miner's black slouch hat. His shirt has a wide Byronic
collar and he wears a sky-blue tie. He is smoking a cigarette. Rings glisten on his fingers. He
is like royalty among his subjects. He dismounts and acknowledges the CROWD with a genial
wave. EVERYONE enjoys the attention they get from being with such a famous man.*

*PEOPLE are clapping and calling out. 'Hey, Oscar! Oscar!' He beams, he takes off his hat
in salute.*

*The MINE OWNER is waiting at the head of the mineshaft, by the large rickety bucket by
which the miners go up and down. He steps forward.*

MINE OWNER

Alright, now let's give a good Colorado welcome here. Hello
sir . . . You're most welcome.

OSCAR

Thank you, thank you.

MINE OWNER
All right everybody, now listen up! I want to introduce you to
Oscar Wilde –

(cheers)

Welcome to the Matchless Silver Mine.
Today we opened up a new seam. We're going to name it after
you.

OSCAR
How very kind. I look forward to collecting the royalties.

This goes down very well.

MINE OWNER
Now, why don't you follow me over here ... Great lecture you
gave last night ... We're truly honoured to have you visit us.

OSCAR sees the bucket. We can see the alarm in his eyes. But he shows none to the CROWD. He steps in and is at once hauled up into the air. For a moment he is a god above the common throng. The CROWD cheers. Guns are fired and hats flung in the air in celebration. And then OSCAR is gone.

2

INTERIOR

Mine Shaft

1882. DAY

OSCAR is hurtling downwards through almost pitch darkness, the bucket clanking and banging down the shaft. It is a dizzying, headlong descent which goes on and on. From what we can see of OSCAR's face, he is quite scared.

3

INTERIOR

Mine Tunnel

1882. DAY

OSCAR is being taken down a tunnel by the MINERS.

OSCAR

I thought I was descending into hell. But with these angel faces to greet me – it must be paradise. Is this the way to my personal seam? Of course, I should have preferred gold. Purple and gold. But we live in a silver age, alas.

4

INTERIOR

Mine Tunnel

1882. DAY

OSCAR is having 'supper' with the MINERS by the seam, which glistens in the rock behind them. 'Supper' consists entirely of whiskey drunk from the bottle. OSCAR addresses the MINERS generally, but one young man, JONES, gets special glancing attention.

OSCAR

So much that is exquisitely beautiful is wrought from suffering, from pain, from toil, broken bones and blistered skin. Benvenuto Cellini understood silver. He took the metal that you mine so nobly down here and transformed it into works of art for popes and princes.

> FIRST MINER

Cellini? Is he a wop?

> OSCAR

A Renaissance man. In every sense. The greatest silversmith the world has ever seen. But a genius in life as well as art. He experimented with every vice known to man, he committed murder —

> JONES

He killed a man?

> OSCAR

More than one.

JONES fills OSCAR's mug from a bottle of whiskey.

> OSCAR *(cont.)*

Thank you.

> FIRST MINER

I'd like to meet this Cellini. Why didn't you bring him with you?

> OSCAR

I'm afraid he's dead.

> JONES

Who shot him?

5

EXTERIOR

London Park

1883. DAY

OSCAR is being driven at a good pace in an open cab.

6

EXTERIOR

Speranza's House

LONDON. 1883. DAY

OSCAR gets out of the cab. He gives the CABMAN a sovereign.

7

INTERIOR

Speranza's House

LONDON. 1883. DAY

Though it is light outside, it is very gloomy in here. SPERANZA, Lady Wilde, OSCAR's mother, is not at all well off, so cannot be fashionable. The curtains are drawn, and the small sitting-room, papered in crimson with gold stars, is lit by red-shaded candles.

SPERANZA is giving an 'at home'. She is in her late fifties, tall and big like OSCAR and very eccentric in dress. Today she is wearing a ten-year-old dress from her days as a Dublin hostess and has her hair down her back. She has a distinct Irish accent.

With her is ADA LEVERSON, a clever, feline writer. She is married and a great friend of OSCAR. She and SPERANZA are watching OSCAR chatting intimately to CONSTANCE LLOYD, a rather serious young woman with great coils of chestnut hair.

ADA

Is Miss Lloyd connected to Lloyd's Bank?

SPERANZA

Ah. No – no.

ADA

Pity.

SPERANZA

But she's comfortable, Ada. A thousand a year.

ADA

Then I congratulate you, Lady Wilde. Now that Oscar's been to America and sown his Wildean oats, it's time he settled down.

OSCAR is talking, CONSTANCE is listening; this is to be the pattern of their relationship, though she is no one's fool.

CONSTANCE

But weren't they very rough?

OSCAR

No, no, charming. Well, charming to me. With each other, it's true, they *could* be a little brusque. They hanged two men in the theatre one night, just before I gave a lecture.

She doesn't know whether to believe him or not. But she is very taken with OSCAR.

OSCAR *(cont.)*

I felt like the sorbet after a side of beef.

They both laugh. They are being watched by LADY MOUNT-TEMPLE, a formidable battleaxe with a lorgnette who has come to join ADA.

LADY MOUNT-TEMPLE

I know your friend is famous, Ada. Notorious, at least. But I don't understand for *what*.

ADA

For being himself, Lady Mount-Temple.

This is not a recommendation to LADY MOUNT-TEMPLE, who frowns. CONSTANCE and OSCAR are unaware of her scrutiny.

CONSTANCE

Don't Americans talk the most wonderful slang, though?

OSCAR

Well, I did hear one lady say: 'After the heel-lick I shifted my day goods.'

CONSTANCE

What on earth did she mean?

OSCAR

She meant that she'd changed her clothes after an afternoon dance.

CONSTANCE laughs again.

SPERANZA comes up with LADY MOUNT-TEMPLE.

SPERANZA

Connie, my love, Lady Mount-Temple is so anxious to meet you.

LADY MOUNT-TEMPLE raises her lorgnette. OSCAR slips away to join ADA.

LADY MOUNT-TEMPLE

I knew your father, Miss Lloyd.

ADA has a sphinx-like smile as she watches. OSCAR lets his mask drop with ADA. He is light and self-mocking. OSCAR and ADA move away.

OSCAR

She's delightful. And not stupid – really, not stupid at all.

ADA still smiles.

ADA

Is that *quite* a reason to marry her?

OSCAR

Well I must marry someone. And my mother has our future planned out in every detail. I'm to go into Parliament. We're to have a nice house, and live a proper settled life. Literature, lectures, the House of Commons – receptions for the world in general at five o'clock –

ADA

How dreary!

OSCAR

Your attendance will not be required at those. But your sphinxiness will be essential for our intimate little dinners at eight.

OSCAR *(cont.)*

(imitates his mother)
It will be a grand life, a charming life.

ADA laughs.

ADA
I see Constance will be busy preparing the dinners. But what will she contribute to the literature and lectures?

OSCAR
She will correct the proofs of my articles.

ADA
Oh, what a little sunbeam!

OSCAR is serious now.
I do love her, Ada. She's —

He can't, for once, find a word.

ADA
Silent? I find her very silent.

OSCAR
But so sympathetic. And I do need an audience.

8

EXTERIOR

London. The Temple

1885. DAY

It is a fine morning, and sunlight dazzles from the windows of the handsome houses where many barristers and solicitors have their offices. OSCAR strides along, humming to himself and sporting a buttonhole and looking very pleased with life. A tide of LAWYERS, some in wigs and gowns, is coming the other way. It parts to let OSCAR through.

9

INTERIOR

Tite Street

STUDY. NIGHT

OSCAR is sitting at a desk, reading. He turns the pages remarkably fast, as though skimming, but he is not. There is a pile of books on the floor beside him.

CONSTANCE comes cautiously in. She watches as OSCAR rapidly turns pages to reach the end of a chapter. Then he looks up and smiles at her.

CONSTANCE

I don't see how you can possibly take it all in.
Reading at that speed.

He holds out the book to her.

OSCAR

Try me.

CONSTANCE

I know better.

OSCAR yawns and sits up.

OSCAR

Where are we dining tonight?

CONSTANCE

At the Leversons'.

OSCAR

Ah, then you must show your true colours.

She looks alarmed.

OSCAR (cont.)

As a propagandist for dress reform.

She is about to protest, but he overrules her.

OSCAR *(cont.)*

The cinnamon cashmere trousers, I think. And – the cape with the ends that turn up into sleeves.

She is shy.

CONSTANCE

I – don't think I can wear those trousers any more.

She means she is pregnant. It takes him a moment to realize, then he jumps to his feet, delighted. He kisses her warmly. Then he imitates his mother.

OSCAR

A new Wilde for the world? Another genius for Ireland?

She nods.

OSCAR *(cont.)*

We shall have to buy you a whole new wardrobe!

She laughs, delighted at his delight.

10

EXTERIOR

Hyde Park

1886. DAY

CONSTANCE is wheeling the baby in his pram past Watt's statue of Physical Energy. ROBERT ROSS is with her, a very intelligent, sharp but small and delicate young man. ADA and OSCAR are behind.

ADA

Ernest proposed to me under that statue.

> OSCAR
>
> Really, the things that go on in front of works of art are quite appalling. The police should interfere.
>
> ADA
>
> We were made not to marry. Whereas you and Constance are so happy — everyone says so.
>
> OSCAR
>
> It's perfectly monstrous how people say things behind one's back that are absolutely true.
>
> ADA
>
> So your audience has proved as responsive as you hoped?
>
> OSCAR
>
> Receptive, yes. Responsive — I always wonder what she's thinking.
>
> ADA
>
> I expect it's about the baby.
>
> OSCAR
>
> Yes ...

She looks at him.

> OSCAR *(cont.)*
>
> Well Constance is such a natural mother, she's invited Robbie into the nest while his parents are abroad.

ADA has her doubts about the wisdom of this. They have now reached CONSTANCE and ROSS.

> OSCAR *(cont.)*
>
> Robbie is Canadian - you can tell by his youth.
>
> ADA
>
> Have you been brought to England to mature, Mr Ross?

ROSS

Well, that was the idea. But it doesn't seem to be working. I've lived here since I was three and you see the pitiful result.

ADA is amused. CONSTANCE ignores all this, cooing to the baby.

OSCAR

Robbie comes from a long line of imperial governors. His grandfather was Prime Minister of Upper Canada. Or was it Lower Canada? The British *will* take their class system with them wherever they go. They apply it even to continents.

ADA

Are *you* planning to govern a continent?

ROSS

Oh, no. I don't even plan to govern myself.

He is young: but not innocent. OSCAR looks at him, meets temptation, resists it. But ADA has seen it.

11

EXTERIOR

West End Department Store

1886. DAY

It is getting dark and carriages are moving slowly because of the crowds. There are many TARTS out already, soliciting. There are also RENTBOYS, male prostitutes, eyeing potential customers.

Through the window of the department store a WINDOW-DRESSER is flirting with a good-looking young RENTBOY as OSCAR and CONSTANCE come out of the main door. CONSTANCE is heavily pregnant now and OSCAR is very solicitous. He hands her the parcels he is carrying.

OSCAR

Could I give you these, my love. I'll see if I can find a cab.

He pushes his way through the CROWD. The RENTBOY, who is very well-spoken, accosts him.

RENTBOY

Looking for someone?

OSCAR is about to ignore him, but the RENTBOY is looking at him so knowingly, so openly, OSCAR can't, for a moment, move. Then he turns away, horrified by his own temptation.

He flags down a cab as though his life depends on it.

OSCAR

Cab! Cab!!!

12

Tite Street

DRAWING ROOM. 1886. NIGHT

CONSTANCE is yawning. ROSS and OSCAR are with her.

CONSTANCE

Bedtime!

ROSS

Just one more cigarette. Oscar?

OSCAR

No – no thanks, Robbie.

CONSTANCE

Don't stay up too late, Robbie.

She kisses him, in a motherly way.

ROSS

Good night. Good night, Oscar.

OSCAR

Good night, Robbie.

OSCAR and CONSTANCE go. ROSS puts the cigarette back in the box. He can wait.

13

INTERIOR

Tite Street

CONSTANCE'S BEDROOM. 1886. NIGHT

OSCAR comes in wearing a dressing-gown over his clothes. CONSTANCE's bedroom has a bath, behind a screen. CONSTANCE is looking at the new baby, VYVYAN, in his cot. She smiles a welcome.

CONSTANCE

Ssh! He's asleep.

He goes and looks at the sleeping baby.

OSCAR

He's so beautiful. Almost as beautiful as his mother. I don't know what I'd do without you, my constant Constance.

He kisses her. She responds. The kiss is surprisingly passionate.

OSCAR *(cont.)*

Good night, my dear.

CONSTANCE

Good night.

He goes out, shutting the door behind him.

14

INTERIOR

Tite Street

CORRIDOR AND STAIRS. 1886. NIGHT

OSCAR looks down the stairs. He hesitates.

15

INTERIOR

Tite Street

DRAWING ROOM. 1886. NIGHT

SAME NIGHT. LATER.

OSCAR and ROSS are alone. The lights are low. It is late. OSCAR paces up and down, talking fast, unusually nervous.

> OSCAR
>
> A university education is an admirable thing, of course. So long as you remember that nothing that is worth knowing can ever be taught. Least of all at Cambridge.

> ROSS
>
> But you told me – in Greece, in ancient Greece, the older men taught the younger. They drew them out. I look forward to being drawn out immensely.

> OSCAR
>
> Yes, well – Greek love – Platonic love – is the highest form of affection known to man, of course.

ROSS

You also told me that the Greeks put statues of Apollo in the bride's chamber, so she would have beautiful sons.

Silence.

ROSS *(cont.)*

I can't help noticing that here the statue's in your bedroom.

OSCAR is hoarse.

OSCAR

Constance prefers a bath.

ROSS laughs. Now he comes boldly over and kisses OSCAR on the lips. OSCAR hesitates only a moment, then kisses him back, with passion. He holds him a moment, then sighs.

OSCAR *(cont.)*

She was so beautiful when I married her, Robbie. Slim, white as a lily, such dancing eyes – I've never seen such love in a pair of eyes, she was –

ROSS slips away and begins to undress.

ROSS

Nothing should reveal the body but the body.

(he smiles)

Didn't you say?

OSCAR's mouth is dry with excitement. ROSS unbuttons his trousers and stands there, waiting.

ROSS *(cont.)*

There has to be a first time for everything, Oscar. Even for you.

OSCAR goes to him.

16

INTERIOR

Tite Street

NURSERY. 1886. DAY

Late afternoon sunlight slants into the nursery where CONSTANCE is feeding VYVYAN, while the NANNY is feeling the water for CYRIL's bath with her elbow. CYRIL is not looking forward to it and crying loudly. OSCAR is watching. He is in evening dress.

> NANNY
>
> Hush, there's a good little fellow. Come on, come on now, there now, come on, Cyril, it's time for your bath. Be a good boy, don't make such a fuss. No, you've got to get undressed, come on. I know you hate it. Boys, Mrs Wilde! They never do what they're told!

> CONSTANCE
>
> We're going to have a girl next time. Aren't we, Oscar?

OSCAR looks at his watch.

> OSCAR
>
> I must go.

He goes and kisses CONSTANCE. He looks at CYRIL who continues to wail.

> OSCAR *(to Constance)*
>
> Goodnight, my dear. Now you behave, Cyril! Remember, a gentleman should take a bath at least once a year!

(he turns casually away)

> I shan't be back till late. I'm dining with the Asquiths.

17

INTERIOR

Hotel Bedroom

1886. NIGHT

OSCAR and ROSS, in bed, finish making love. OSCAR has kept most of his clothes on. ROSS has his eyes closed, his head resting on OSCAR's shoulder. OSCAR kisses him on the lips, a quick, affectionate kiss. ROSS opens his eyes and smiles.

> ROSS
>
> Do you love me?

> OSCAR
>
> I feel like a city that's been under siege for twenty years, and suddenly the gates are thrown open and the citizens come pouring out –

ROSS giggles.

> OSCAR *(cont.)*
>
> – to breathe the air and walk the fields and pluck the wild flowers –

ROSS giggles again, but feels very happy.

> OSCAR *(cont.)*
>
> I feel *relieved.*

> ROSS
>
> You don't worry about Constance?

OSCAR thinks seriously. He looks away, unable to answer.

18

INTERIOR

Tite Street

NURSERY. 1889. DAY

*OSCAR is repairing damage to CYRIL's fort, sticking soldiers together which
have got broken. CYRIL, now four, is watching intently. VYVYAN, three, sits on
CONSTANCE's knee.*

OSCAR

Every afternoon, on their way home from school, the children
used to play in the garden of the selfish giant.

CYRIL

Is that the garden where we go and play?

OSCAR

No, darling, this one's much larger and lovelier than that, with
soft green grass and –

CYRIL

There's grass where we go.

OSCAR

Ah yes, but are there twelve peach trees that burst into delicate
blossoms of pink and pearl every springtime, and bear rich fruit
in the autumn?

CYRIL looks to CONSTANCE.

CYRIL

Are there, Mama?

CONSTANCE

I don't think there are, Cyril, no.

OSCAR

Would you hand me a matchstick, darling, and I'll put this Hussar's head back on.

CYRIL gives him the matchstick. OSCAR resumes his story.

OSCAR *(cont.)*

The birds sat on the trees and sang so sweetly that the children used to stop their games to listen. 'How happy we are here!' they said to each other.

CYRIL

I don't know how they could be happy if there was a giant.

OSCAR

Ah, but there wasn't, you see. Not yet. He was away, visiting a friend.

CYRIL

You're always away.

OSCAR *concentrates on the soldier he's mending.*

OSCAR

Yes, but I only go for a night or two at a time. And I always come back. Whereas this giant, the one whose garden it was, he'd been away for seven years, staying with an ogre in Cornwall. And after seven years he'd said all he had to say, because his conversation was very limited –

CONSTANCE *laughs.* OSCAR *looks quickly up and gives a grateful smile.*

OSCAR *(cont.)*

He decided to return home to his own castle. And when he arrived and found the children playing in his garden, he was very angry.

(puts on a very gruff voice)

'What are you doing here?' he cried. And all the children ran away. 'My own garden is my own garden,' said the giant, 'and I won't allow anyone to play in it except myself.' So he built a high wall, all round, and put up a large notice board on which was written in capital letters: TRESPASSERS WILL BE PROSECUTED.

There is a knock at the door and ARTHUR, *the footman, appears.*

OSCAR *(cont.)*

Arthur, you're trespassing. Cyril will now eat you.

ARTHUR

It's Mr Ross, sir, with Mr Gray.

OSCAR *abandons the soldiers at once.*

Good Heavens, I must fly. The horses of Apollo are pawing impatiently at the gates.

CYRIL

I beg your pardon?

OSCAR *kisses* CYRIL *quickly, anxious to be off.*

OSCAR

Papa must go.

CYRIL

You will come back and finish the story?

OSCAR

Of course I will.

CONSTANCE

Now come on, Cyril. It's almost tea-time.

19

INTERIOR

Art Gallery

1889. DAY

A private view of an exhibition of modern portraits. PEOPLE are, as today, drinking and talking and not looking at the pictures. They are looking, however, at OSCAR, ROSS and JOHN GRAY, a handsome young poet, who are themselves looking at a picture by a Pre-Raphaelite artist of a beautiful young woman.

GRAY

I really don't know why people bother painting portraits any more. You can get a much better likeness with a photograph.

ROSS

Oh, but a photograph's just one moment in time, one gesture, one turn of the head.

OSCAR

Yes, portraits are not likenesses, Mr Gray. Painters show the soul of the subject, the essence.

GRAY
The essence of the sitter's vanity, you mean.
ROSS
Well, this is a portrait of Lady Battersby as a young woman.
She's over there, as a matter of fact. I must go and console her.

He goes over to a wrinkled old LADY BATTERSBY. GRAY looks from her to the portrait and back again.

> GRAY
>
> Poor thing. I expect in her heart she thinks she still looks like this.

He looks at the picture, sad. OSCAR is looking at him, not sad at all.

> GRAY *(cont.)*
>
> If we could look young and innocent forever –
>
> OSCAR
>
> Do you think we'd want to?
>
> GRAY
>
> If our souls were ugly, yes.

An idea is catching hold.

> OSCAR
>
> Give a man a mask and he'll tell you the truth. Have we had enough of this? Shall we go and have dinner somewhere?

GRAY is flattered and delighted. ROSS watches them go. He is fond of OSCAR but quite unsentimental about their relationship. He smiles as he sees OSCAR's arm go round GRAY's shoulder.

20

INTERIOR

London Hotel

SUITE. 1889. NIGHT

OSCAR and JOHN GRAY are in the bedroom. There is an open bottle of champagne on a table, and two half-filled glasses. Once again, OSCAR has kept most of his clothes on, though GRAY, slim and beautiful, has not.

GRAY lies back to let OSCAR gaze upon him. GRAY stretches up and pulls OSCAR down onto the bed.

21

INTERIOR

INTERIOR

Speranza's House

HALL/DRAWING ROOM. 1890. DAY

CONSTANCE has come in some distress to see SPERANZA. The curtains are drawn though it's the middle of the day. SPERANZA is ecstatic and unhelpful.

SPERANZA

Dorian Gray is the most wonderful book I've ever read. The end, when the servants break in and they find him wizened, old and dead, and the picture young again – I fainted!

CONSTANCE

My family say it's dull and wicked.

SPERANZA

Dull! Oh, it's sublime! It's about the masks we wear as faces, and the faces we wear as masks. That my son should have written a work of such ...

CONSTANCE

People say it's full of dangerous paradoxes. Hardly anyone will speak to us any more. We're ceasing to be respectable.

SPERANZA stares at her, then tosses her mane of hair.

SPERANZA

Artists care nothing about respectability. It's only jealousy! It's the spite of the untalented for the man of genius!

(changes the subject)

Where is Oscar?

CONSTANCE

He's in the Lake District. Writing a play.

SPERANZA

A drama!

CONSTANCE

A comedy.

SPERANZA is thrilled.

CONSTANCE *(cont.)*

Robbie Ross has gone to keep him company. I do like Robbie.

SPERANZA

And they both love you. Oh, it'll be a great success! Oscar is made for the stage!

22

EXTERIOR

St James's Theatre

1892. NIGHT

It is the opening night of Lady Windermere's Fan. *Cabs and carriages are lined up for the end of the play. There is a huge burst of applause for the final curtain.*

23

INTERIOR

St James's Theatre

1892. NIGHT

We are backstage with the ACTORS going on to take their bows. The applause is loud and long. The curtain goes up, comes down, goes up.

OSCAR is watching in the wings, very nervous. He is wearing a green carnation, and carries a lit cigarette in a mauve-gloved hand. The curtain rises and falls. There are louder and louder cries for the author. OSCAR prepares himself.

He puts on his mask of total confidence. He saunters on. The applause redoubles. He takes the centre of the stage.

OSCAR

Ladies and gentlemen, I have enjoyed this evening *immensely.*

Laughter.

OSCAR *(cont.)*

The actors have given us a *charming* rendering of a *delightful* play, and your appreciation has been most intelligent.

I congratulate you on the great success of your performance, which persuades me that you think *almost* as highly of this play as I do myself.

He bows, and the applause breaks out again.

24

St James's Theatre

BAR. NIGHT

A first-night party is under way, with all the ACTORS and ACTRESSES, and many YOUNG MEN wearing green carnations. ROSS is there, and LIONEL JOHNSON, a diminutive alcoholic poet, with his very beautiful cousin, LORD ALFRED DOUGLAS, universally known as BOSIE. OSCAR is greeted as he comes in by JOHN GRAY.

> GRAY
> It went so well, Oscar, even better than I'd –
> They loved it, they absolutely loved it.

> OSCAR
> And I, dear boy, love you.

He finds ADA with ROSS.

> ADA
> Oscar ...

> OSCAR
> Sphinx!

> ADA
> You really must be careful. You're in grave danger of becoming rich.

ROSS

It was wonderful. As I knew it would be.

OSCAR

Thank you, Robbie.

ROSS

Everyone's dying to know who the real Lady Windermere is.

OSCAR

The real Lady Windermere is every woman in this room, and most of the men.

LIONEL JOHNSON approaches.

JOHNSON

Oscar. It's a wonderful play. My cousin Lord Alfred Douglas is here. He would very much like to congratulate you.

He turns, smiling, to find BOSIE. BOSIE looks at OSCAR with a mixture of arrogance and admiration that, added to his beauty, OSCAR finds quite dazzling.

JOHNSON

Oscar, this is Bosie Douglas.

But it's as though he's not there. BOSIE and OSCAR are looking one another in the eyes.

BOSIE

We met last year. Lionel brought me to tea at Tite Street.

OSCAR

How could I possibly forget?

BOSIE is not afraid of him at all.

BOSIE

I love your play. The audience didn't know whether you meant your jokes or not. You shocked them, especially with your speech. But the more frivolous you seem, the more serious you are, aren't you? I love that.

OSCAR

Thank you. I always say, the young are the only critics with enough experience to judge my work.

BOSIE

We need shocking. People are so banal. And you use your wit like a foil — you cut right through all those starched shirt-fronts. You draw blood. It's magnificent.

OSCAR is very gratified; and impressed.

BOSIE *(cont.)*

I wish you'd draw some blood down in Oxford. Though you'd need a miracle. All the dons at my college have dust in their veins.

OSCAR laughs, delighted.

OSCAR

Ah. At which college do you educate the fellows?

BOSIE

Magdalen.

OSCAR

My own College. Well, I shall claim the privilege of a graduate and come and take tutorials with you.

BOSIE

Come soon, then. They're threatening to send me down.

OSCAR

How could they be so cruel to one so beautiful?

BOSIE

Dons. They're so middle-class.

GRAY has been watching the exchange with some anxiety. GEORGE ALEXANDER, the actor-manager, is coming up.

ALEXANDER

My dear Oscar, you've shocked the whole of London, smoking on stage like that.

BOSIE thinks this is pathetic. OSCAR sees this and is delighted.

OSCAR

Excellent, then we shall run for a year!

GRAY

Oscar, you must say something to Marion Terry.

We see the ACTRESS across the room. OSCAR's attention is still for BOSIE.

OSCAR

She was good, wasn't she? So good, in fact, that I think she wrote most of the lines herself.

BOSIE laughs. Their eyes are locked.

OSCAR *(cont.)*

Excuse me, Lord Alfred.

BOSIE

Bosie – please.

OSCAR

Bosie.

Then OSCAR moves. GRAY is looking very unhappy.

25

INTERIOR

Tite Street

NURSERY. 1892. DAY

CONSTANCE is reading to the children, now seven and six, from OSCAR's now published story.

CONSTANCE

'My own garden is my own garden,' said the giant. So he built a high wall all around it and put up a notice board: TRESPASSERS WILL BE PROSECUTED. He was a very selfish giant. The poor

CONSTANCE (*cont.*)

children had now nowhere to play. They tried to play on the road, but the road was very dusty and full of hard stones, and they did not like it. They used to wander round the high wall of the giant's garden when their lessons were over, and talk about the beautiful garden inside.'

26

EXTERIOR

Magdalen College – River

1892. DAY

OSCAR and BOSIE are walking arm-in-arm beside the river in Magdalen College garden. We hear CONSTANCE still reading the story.

CONSTANCE(o/s)

'How happy we were there!' they said to each other.

OSCAR

I hope he was a very *beautiful* boy?

BOSIE

Well – pretty, you know, in a street arab sort of way

He wants to sound sophisticated, but is really quite insecure.

OSCAR

There's no point being blackmailed by an ugly one.

BOSIE

What's tiresome is, he's – he's threatening to show my letters to my father.

OSCAR

Who will show them to all his friends, I'm sure, for the excellence of their style.

BOSIE's sophistication goes. He becomes an unhappy little boy.

BOSIE

No. No. You don't know him. He's a brute. Really. He carries a whip wherever he goes. He used to beat my mother, he beat my brothers. He thrashed me from the age …

He shivers. OSCAR is shocked. He puts an arm round him.

OSCAR

My dear boy –

BOSIE recovers some of his bravado.

BOSIE

Of course, he's practically illiterate, he probably won't understand the letters anyway.

OSCAR laughs.

OSCAR

By an unforgivable oversight, I've never been blackmailed myself, but my friends assure me that a hundred pounds will usually suffice.

BOSIE's sophistication vanishes in relief.

BOSIE

Really? God, you promise?

OSCAR

Leave it to Lewis. George Lewis, my solicitor. He knows what he's doing. He acts for the Prince of Wales.

They stroll on together.

27

INTERIOR

Bosie's Room

OXFORD. 1892. DAY

BOSIE has a piano in his rooms. A FRIEND is accompanying him as he sings 'Ah, Leave me not to Pine Alone' from The Pirates of Penzance *by Gilbert and Sullivan. He has a charming voice and OSCAR is enchanted. There is a small audience of BOSIE's FRIENDS, very impressed that OSCAR is there.*

UNDERGRADUATE
Isn't he killing, Mr Wilde?

OSCAR is completely sincere.

OSCAR
He's perfect. He's perfect in every way.

He is in an enchanted world.

28

INTERIOR

Bosie's Room

OXFORD. 1892. NIGHT

OSCAR and BOSIE have made love and lie in each other's arms. Later, OSCAR gazes at BOSIE, asleep.

29

INTERIOR

Oxford Hotel

DINING-ROOM. 1892. DAY

The HEAD WAITER is showing OSCAR and BOSIE to a table at the side of the restaurant.

> BOSIE
> I don't want to sit here. I want to sit *there.*

He points to a table in the middle of the room.

The HEAD WAITER looks at OSCAR.

> OSCAR
> You heard what Lord Alfred said.

> BOSIE
> I want everyone to look at us.

The HEAD WAITER bows and shows them to the centre table. As they sit down BOSIE speaks very clearly.

> BOSIE
> I want everyone to say, Look, there's Oscar Wilde with his boy.

OSCAR beams his delight at this deliberate provocation. He is in love both with BOSIE and his daring.

The HEAD WAITER has continued to spread their napkins for them as though he hasn't heard a word.

> OSCAR
> So, what shall we let people see us eating?

> BOSIE
> Foie gras and lobster. And champagne.

OSCAR closes the menu and smiles at the WAITER.

OSCAR

For two. We do everything together.

WAITER

Very good, Mr Wilde.

PEOPLE are beginning to look already.

LATER:

To one side, TWO WAITERS confer in whispers with the HEAD WAITER. The restaurant is deserted now, but for OSCAR and BOSIE.

BOSIE

I think he enjoyed thrashing me. All my family are mad. My uncle slit his throat last year. In a railway hotel.

OSCAR

Which station?

BOSIE

Euston.

OSCAR

Ah, all life's really serious journeys involve a railway terminus.

(he looks at his watch)

And now I must go to the station myself.

(he smiles lovingly at BOSIE)

Sarah Bernhardt thinks she knows better than I do how to play Salome.

BOSIE

Stay. Please stay. At least – at least till this evening.

OSCAR hesitates only a moment.

OSCAR

Sarah is divine, as you are. She will be wonderful at the play's climax, when Salome kisses the lips of the severed head of John the Baptist.

OSCAR *(cont.)*

(begins to act it out)

'Ah, thou wouldst not suffer me to kiss thy mouth, Jokanaan.' Jokanaan is an old Hebrew name for John. 'Well, I will kiss it now. I will bite it with my teeth as one bites a ripe fruit. Yes, I will kiss thy mouth, Jokanaan.

BOSIE is enthralled.

OSCAR *(cont.)*

Thy body is white like the snows that lie on the mountains ...'

30

INTERIOR

Bosie's Room

OXFORD. 1892. NIGHT

BOSIE is naked, standing with his back to the camera. OSCAR is watching him. We continue to hear OSCAR's voice over.

OSCAR

'...like the snows that lie on the mountains of Judaea, and come down into the valleys. The roses in the garden of the Queen of Arabia are not so white as thy body.'

BOSIE turns and smiles, shy. He loves OSCAR.

31

INTERIOR

Cheshire Cheese

PUB. 1892. NIGHT

ROSS and GRAY are at the bar.

GRAY
I'm not good enough for him any more. I'm just the son of a carpenter, while Bosie —

ROSS
Oscar's only ever been smitten before. He was smitten with me, he was smitten with you —

GRAY
I wasn't *smitten*. I *loved* him.

ROSS
Well — now he's fallen in love.

GRAY is wretched.

GRAY
I'm halfway to hell-fire. I'm not joking.

ROSS is genuinely sympathetic.

ROSS
Someone else was a carpenter's son.

GRAY is startled.

ROSS *(cont.)*
I've given in and become a Catholic. I find confession wonderfully consoling.

GRAY
I can't go to confession when I — want to kill Bosie.
Or myself.

32

EXTERIOR

Babbacombe Beach

1892. DAY

CYRIL and VYVYAN are playing on the sands, supervised by their NANNY.

CONSTANCE(o/s)

Oscar's furious.

LADY MOUNT-TEMPLE (o/s)

He has no right to be. He knew perfectly well the Lord Chamberlain would never allow a play with biblical characters. He never has done.

We find CONSTANCE in the shelter of a sea-wall. Sitting with her under a parasol is LADY MOUNT-TEMPLE.

CONSTANCE

Oscar doesn't think there should be censorship of plays at all.

LADY MOUNT-TEMPLE

Well, of course there must be censorship. Or people would say what they meant, and then where should we be? When is he coming to join us?

CONSTANCE

He's not. He must stay and look after Lord Alfred.

LADY MOUNT-TEMPLE

Those Douglases are always ill. When they're not demented. One of them, you know, he roasted a kitchen-boy on a spit.

CONSTANCE looks alarmed.

LADY MOUNT-TEMPLE*(cont.)*
And Bosie's father – Lord Queensberry. Oh, he's a dreadful
man, Constance. Doesn't believe in God. Or marriage. A
Marquess should set a proper example or what are the upper
classes for? I tell you, I wouldn't want a daughter of mine to
marry a Douglas.

Silence.

                        CONSTANCE
I haven't got a daughter.
                    LADY MOUNT-TEMPLE
Plenty of time still, my dear.

CONSTANCE shakes her head.

                    LADY MOUNT-TEMPLE*(cont.)*
Oh. Oh, I see!

CONSTANCE is embarrassed.

                        CONSTANCE
It's – my fault. After Vyvyan was born, all I could think of was
the children.
                    LADY MOUNT-TEMPLE
Ah.

Silence.

                    LADY MOUNT-TEMPLE*(cont.)*
So that's why Oscar spends so much time with his men friends.
                        CONSTANCE
Oscar needs disciples. And Lord Alfred's a poet,
a very fine poet, Oscar says.

LADY MOUNT-TEMPLE looks doubtful.

                        CONSTANCE*(cont.)*
He's studying Classics. Oscar and he, they talk about Plato and
so on.

LADY MOUNT-TEMPLE raises her eyebrows. CONSTANCE is beginning to feel rattled.

> CONSTANCE *(cont.)*
> There's nothing wrong, really there isn't.
> LADY MOUNT-TEMPLE
> It's not whether there *is* anything wrong. It's whether or not there appears to be. That's all people care about. The Empire was not built by men like Bosie Douglas.

We hear OSCAR reading over.

> OSCAR (o/s)
> Then the spring came, and all over the country there were little blossoms and little birds.

33

EXTERIOR

Tite Street

NURSERY WINDOW. 1893. DAY

CYRIL and VYVYAN are standing at the nursery window, looking out through the bars for their absent father. We hear OSCAR continuing the story over.

> OSCAR (o/s)
> Only in the garden of the selfish giant it was still winter. The birds did not care to sing in it as there were no children, and the trees forgot to blossom. The snow covered up the grass with her great white cloak, and the frost painted all the trees silver.

34

INTERIOR

London Hotel

SUITE. 1893. NIGHT

BOSIE is lying on a sofa in the sitting-room, reading. He looks very beautiful.

OSCAR comes from the bedroom and leans against the door. He looks at BOSIE longingly. But BOSIE's not in the mood. OSCAR sits beside him and starts to undo his shirt. BOSIE lets him, he doesn't want to be unkind. But he gives him a long deep look, as though he's away in some private world, and doesn't want distraction.

OSCAR can't meet his eye. He kisses his naked breast and throat. BOSIE turns his head and they kiss. Then BOSIE jumps up, goes to a mirror and starts tidying his hair and buttoning his shirt.

BOSIE

Let's go out.

OSCAR

If you like.

35

EXTERIOR

London

1893. NIGHT

A cab races by.

WILDE

36

EXTERIOR

London

1893. NIGHT

OSCAR is pretending to be more cheerful than he is. BOSIE enjoys being more knowing about something than OSCAR.

> BOSIE
> The thing about renters is, you don't have to consider their feelings.

> OSCAR
> Oh, but if someone is willing to give one pleasure, one should show gratitude at least.

> BOSIE
> No. Money, that's all they want. What's wonderful about going to Taylor's is, no one pretends. You just do it and be done with it.

(he looks seriously at OSCAR)

> I do love you, Oscar but – variety is the spice of life.

BOSIE kisses him and takes his hand and smiles.

> BOSIE *(cont.)*
> You can watch me, if you like.

37

INTERIOR

Taylor's Flat

WESTMINSTER. 1893. NIGHT

ALFRED TAYLOR is young, and getting through a fortune as fast as he can, with the help of YOUNG MEN, two of whom are present: CHARLES PARKER and ALFRED WOOD. There is food and drink. BOSIE is introducing the BOYS to OSCAR.

> BOSIE
>
> Alfred Taylor – this is Oscar.

> WOOD
>
> Hello, Oscar.

He grins, seeing a victim. OSCAR offers him one of his elaborately tipped cigarettes.

> OSCAR
>
> Do you smoke?

> WOOD
>
> Oh, I do everything.

> TAYLOR
>
> Expertly, I might add.

OSCAR takes out a cigarette, lights it, then hands one to WOOD.

> WOOD *(cont.)*
>
> Nice case!

OSCAR hands it to him.

> OSCAR
>
> I want you to keep it.

(he looks round)

> So this is a den of vice. I should call it more of a garden. Such pretty flowers, Mr Taylor. How wise of you to keep the curtains closed. They would never grow in the light of common day.

WOOD

'Ere, who are you calling common?

OSCAR

Certainly not you, dear boy. You seem to be a flower of the very rarest hue. Bosie never told me that you were a botanist, Mr Taylor. That you roam the earth, climbing the highest peaks of the Himalayas, and plunging into the darkest forests of Borneo, to return triumphant to this delightful conservatory in the shadow of Westminster Abbey, to exhibit your specimens.

TAYLOR

The boys are all Londoners, actually.

OSCAR

Impossible. I see Londoners every day, but never such exotic blooms as these.

WOOD

Does he always talk like this?

BOSIE

Not when he's in bed.

He makes a gesture implying that OSCAR has his mouth full. WOOD laughs, TAYLOR laughs, ALLEN laughs. We hear ROSS over this.

38

INTERIOR

Tite Street

DRAWING ROOM. 1893. DAY

ROSS

I am discreet. Bosie of course is far too grand and well-born for that. He wants everyone to know. Oscar, you must understand . . .

OSCAR

I must be with young people, Robbie. They're so frank and free and — they make me feel young myself.

ROSS

That's all very well, but what would you say if someone wanted to go to bed with *your* son?

OSCAR is surprised and shocked.

> OSCAR
>
> Cyril's eight.

> ROSS
>
> What will you say when he's eighteen?

OSCAR has to think seriously.

> Nothing. He must do as his nature dictates. As I only wish I'd done.

39

EXTERIOR

Goring on Thames

1893. DAY

It is a lovely summer day, and OSCAR is wading near a small jetty. CYRIL and VYVYAN have fishing nets and are catching small minnows. OSCAR is carrying on with the story of The Selfish Giant. The boys know it by heart now, and love it all the more for that.

> OSCAR
>
> 'I do believe the spring has come at last,' said the giant, and he jumped out of bed and looked out of the window.

CYRIL and VYVYAN speak with OSCAR.

> CYRIL
>
> And what did he see?

> OSCAR
>
> Ah, you tell me.

> CYRIL
>
> No, you tell it.

OSCAR

Alright. He saw the most wonderful sight. Through a little hole in the wall the children had crept back into the garden, and were sitting on the branches of the trees. And on every tree that he could see there was a little child. And the trees were so glad that —

CYRIL

They'd covered themselves with blossoms —

VYVYAN

Blossoms.

OSCAR

— and were waving their arms gently above the children's heads. And the birds were twittering and singing above them with delight.

CONSTANCE approaches.

OSCAR *(cont.)*

And the flowers were looking up through the grass and laughing.

CONSTANCE

Oscar! It's time the boys changed. We'll miss the train!

OSCAR

Ah. Come on boys.

CYRIL

Oh, Papa, can't we stay?

CONSTANCE

Papa's got to *work*. He's got to finish his play.

OSCAR grimaces.

OSCAR

Yes. Poor Papa!

CYRIL/VYVYAN

Poor Papa, poor, poor, poor, poor, poor Papa.

40

EXTERIOR

Goring House

STUDY. 1893. DAY

OSCAR is sitting at his desk, writing his new play. We hear the sounds of laughter coming through the open window.

41

EXTERIOR

Goring House

LAWN. 1893. DAY

The house OSCAR has rented has lawns running down to the river. BOSIE is playing badminton with a group of OXFORD FRIENDS. They are drinking champagne between shots.

FIRST FRIEND

Where is Oscar? We haven't seen him at all.

BOSIE

Where do you think he is? He's working. He is a writer, after all.

FIRST FRIEND

I hear your father's threatening to shoot Lord Rosebery.

BOSIE

Really? He usually prefers the horsewhip.

FIRST FRIEND

Says he's been buggering your brother.

> BOSIE
>
> Well – Rosebery *is* Secretary of State for Foreign Affairs. And Francis is his *private* secretary.

They all laugh.

> BOSIE *(cont.)*
>
> Actually Francis is about to get engaged ...
>
> SECOND FRIEND
>
> What's your father talking about, then?
>
> BOSIE
>
> Oh, he's obsessed with sex. He thinks Oscar's buggering *me*. As though I'd allow anyone to do that.

42

INTERIOR

Goring House

STUDY. 1893. DAY

OSCAR is at his desk, writing. BOSIE is lolling in the doorway, bored and spoiling for a fight.

> BOSIE
>
> I'm sick of the country.

OSCAR doesn't respond.

> BOSIE *(cont.)*
>
> Let's go back to London.

(pause)

> Well, what's the point of us living together if you're always working?

OSCAR

I have responsibilities, a wife and family, I –

BOSIE

Oh, God, not that again! I ask my friends over from Oxford, and you just disappear! I'd be better off staying at my mother's – at least she's *there*.

OSCAR

Bosie, you asked me specially to take this house so that we –

BOSIE

Well, now I'm bored with it! And with you!

OSCAR

I can't give it up. It's paid for in advance. Until I finish my new –

BOSIE just sniffs.

OSCAR *(cont.)*

Bosie, dear – you have beauty, you have breeding, and, most glorious of all, you have youth. But you are very fantastical if you think that pleasures don't have to be earned and paid for.

BOSIE

Whenever I want to do anything, you say you can't afford it. But you give all those renters cigarette cases.

OSCAR is flabbergasted. He is the most generous of men.

OSCAR

But I've *lavished* presents on you. Every penny I've earned from my play I have spent on you.

BOSIE

Oh, I'm sure you've been *counting!*

This is outrageous, and he knows it, and doesn't care.

BOSIE *(cont.)*

You're so mean and penny-pinching and middle-class, all you can think about is your *bank* balance.

OSCAR

Bosie, for God's sake, this is intolerable!

BOSIE

No gentleman ever has the slightest idea what his bank balance is! You're absurd! Telling everyone how they ought to live – You're so *vulgar* – I never want to see you again! Ever!

OSCAR

All right, then, go! If that's what you want, then go! Go on, go. Get out! Get out!

BOSIE storms out.

POV SHOT of BOSIE running away, and we hear CYRIL's voice over continuing the story of The Selfish Giant *by heart, with a few hesitations and mistakes.*

CYRIL (O/S)

But in the farthest corner of the garden
it was still winter, and in it was standing a little boy.
He was so small he could not reach up to
the branches of the tree. 'Climb up, little boy!'
said the tree, but the little boy was too tiny.

43

EXTERIOR

Lady Queensberry's House

1893. DAY

A carriage is waiting, piled high with luggage. Someone is going away for a long time.

44

INTERIOR

Lady Queensberry's House

1893. DAY

LADY QUEENSBERRY is with BOSIE. He is dressed for travelling. They are walking through the house towards the front door.

LADY QUEENSBERRY

Egypt is lovely this time of year. You mustn't idle your time away.

BOSIE

Mother –

LADY QUEENSBERRY

And I want you to promise me something.

They stop and face one another.

LADY QUEENSBERRY *(cont.)*

Not to write to Oscar Wilde.

BOSIE

I can't do that.

LADY QUEENSBERRY

Bosie –

BOSIE is for once completely genuine.

BOSIE

I love Oscar.

She is too horrified to speak.

LADY QUEENSBERRY

But he's not fit to teach anything – he's – he's evil!

BOSIE

Do you really think your own son could love someone evil? I just wish I could love Oscar as loyally, devotedly, unselfishly and purely as he loves me.

She is silent.

BOSIE*(cont.)*

But I'm not as good as he is. I probably never will be.

(he kisses her)

Goodbye, then.

He turns and goes. She stays where she is.

45

Haymarket Theatre

1893. DAY

A rehearsal of A Woman of No Importance *is in progress: LORD ILLINGWORTH and MRS ALLONBY at the end of Act One. Watching from the stalls are OSCAR, ADA and ROSS. HERBERT BEERBOHM TREE, the actor-manager and director, is near the front.*

ILLINGWORTH
I adore simple pleasures. They are the last refuge of the complex. But, if you wish, let us stay here. Yes, let us stay here. The Book of Life begins with a man and a woman in a garden.

MRS ALLONBY
It ends with Revelations.

ADA laughs, but OSCAR rises.

OSCAR
Ahm, yes, Mr Tree ... may I ...?

OSCAR speaks to the ACTORS.

OSCAR
I'm delighted, of course, that you find my lines funny. But please don't try and make the audience laugh with them. They should sound completely spontaneous and natural, as though people spoke like that all the time.

TREE
Yes, of course. Let's try again.

OSCAR smiles and retreats back to his stall while TREE confers with the ACTORS.

ADA

You should break with Bosie more often, Oscar. Then we'd have more of your spontaneous and natural plays.

OSCAR smiles, with some difficulty.

ROSS

Bosie was envious. That's why he stopped Oscar working.

OSCAR

Robbie – please – that's not true –

ROSS

Of course it is. His poems aren't nearly as good as you pretend, and he knows it. He's just a shallow little …

ADA

Rivulet.

Silence.

OSCAR

Bosie is a *child* – a vulnerable child. He needs love.

ADA

Oh, we all *need* love. But which of us can give it?

46

INTERIOR

Tite Street

DINING-ROOM. 1893. NIGHT

It is Christmas and OSCAR, CONSTANCE, CYRIL and VYVYAN are pulling crackers. It is a happy family party. There is a Christmas tree with a fairy on top. We hear OSCAR going on with the story of The Selfish Giant.

OSCAR (o/s)
And the giant's heart melted as he looked out.
'How selfish I have been!' he said. 'Now I know why
the spring would not come here. I will put that little
boy on top of the tree, and I will knock down the wall,
and my garden shall be the children's playground for
ever and ever.' He was really very sorry for what
he had done.

47

INTERIOR

Tite Street

NURSERY. 1893. NIGHT

OSCAR and CONSTANCE are putting the BOYS to bed.
OSCAR (v/o)
So he crept downstairs and opened the front door
quite softly, and went out into the garden.
The little boy did not run away, for his eyes were
so full of tears that he did not see the giant
coming. And the giant stole up behind
him and took him gently by the hand and
put him up into the tree.
OSCAR and CONSTANCE kiss the BOYS good night.
OSCAR (v/o *cont.*)
And the tree broke at once into blossom,
and the birds came and sang on it, and the little
boy stretched out his two arms and flung
them round the giant's neck and kissed him.

48

EXTERIOR

Backstreet

1894. NIGHT

A carriage speeds along.

49

INTERIOR

Savoy Hotel

RECEPTION. 1894. NIGHT

BOSIE followed by PORTERS carrying his luggage, rushes through reception and runs up the stairs.

50

INTERIOR

Savoy Hotel

SUITE. 1894. NIGHT

OSCAR and BOSIE hug each other deliriously.

BOSIE

Oscar! I don't care what people think, I love you. I love you! It's all that matters to me in the world. It was agony being away from you. Well … here I am.

The door is open and the PORTERS arrive with the luggage. They stand and stare.
OSCAR and BOSIE are oblivious.

> OSCAR
>
> Oh Bosie, you're my catastrophe. My doom. Everyone says so, even me.

> BOSIE
>
> I missed you.

51

INTERIOR

Café Royal

1894. DAY

OSCAR is handing BOSIE a small parcel.

> OSCAR
>
> I thought you might like something to celebrate your return.

BOSIE unwraps it eagerly. It is a pair of emerald cuff-links.

> BOSIE
>
> Oscar!

He is as pleased as a child.

> OSCAR
>
> When I saw them in the window, they begged me on their knees to make them yours.

> BOSIE
>
> I'll put them on now! They're superb!

He starts to undo the links he has on, then suddenly looks across the room to where someone is creating a scene. It is his father, the MARQUESS OF QUEENSBERRY.

QUEENSBERRY

No, no, no, no, I'll sit there! I want a proper table!

The HEAD WAITER comes hurrying over.

HEAD WAITER

Is there something wrong, my lord?

QUEENSBERRY

Of course there is! This young fool wants me to sit by the service door!

BOSIE has gone pale.

BOSIE

Oh God. My father!

OSCAR turns and sees QUEENSBERRY. QUEENSBERRY is being shown to a better table.

HEAD WAITER

I'm extremely sorry, my lord, he's new, he didn't know who you were.

QUEENSBERRY

Give me the menu.

BOSIE rises.

OSCAR

Bosie, you're not going to flee?

BOSIE doesn't answer. OSCAR watches with apprehension as BOSIE goes over to his father. QUEENSBERRY doesn't look up, thinking he's a waiter.

QUEENSBERRY

I'll have the pea soup, then the salmon.

BOSIE

Will you have it with us, Papa?

QUEENSBERRY

Bosie!

BOSIE

I'm lunching with Oscar Wilde. Will you join us?

QUEENSBERRY is at once ready to go into one of his tirades.

QUEENSBERRY

I told you never to see that vile cur again.

BOSIE

He's not vile or a cur, he's utterly delightful. Come and see.

OSCAR is peering round his menu to see how BOSIE is doing.

BOSIE *(cont.)*

How do you know what he's like when you've never met him? Come on, Papa. You're not a man to be influenced by other people's opinions.

This goes home. QUEENSBERRY rises. BOSIE is very conscious of everyone watching as they cross the restaurant to OSCAR.

BOSIE *(cont.)*

Oscar, you – you've never met my father, have you?

OSCAR rises. The two MEN shake hands.

OSCAR

Lord Queensberry – Bosie has told me so much about your exploits on the race-track.

They sit.

OSCAR *(cont.)*

I've never heard such bad luck as yours with the Grand National. Bosie tells me that you would have won, but that your cousin wouldn't let you ride the horse.

QUEENSBERRY is melting already.

QUEENSBERRY

Bloody fool said I was too old. Well, you're never too old. Besides I'd ridden Old Joe on the gallops. Came in at forty to one.

BOSIE is appreciating OSCAR's tactfulness.

OSCAR

No horse could ever have carried me over the jumps, I fear. What are you having?

QUEENSBERRY

Pea soup, and salmon.

OSCAR

Then I shall join you. Spring is the time to lunch on salmon. Though I always think it tastes so much nicer if you've caught it yourself.

QUEENSBERRY

You fish?

He is very surprised.

OSCAR

I used to. When I lived in Ireland. My father had the most charming hunting lodge on an island in a lake. Do you know the west of Ireland?

QUEENSBERRY

Not really. Whereabouts, exactly?

52

INTERIOR

Café Royal

VESTIBULE. 1894. DAY

BOSIE comes out of the restaurant, smiling to himself. SOMEONE hurries up and helps him on with his coat. He glances back into the restaurant, laughs and goes.

53

INTERIOR

Café Royal

1894. DAY

*Almost all the other lunchers have left, but OSCAR and QUEENSBERRY are smoking
cigars and discussing Christianity over their brandy.*

QUEENSBERRY

The Christians, they go around pretending they know who
God is and how he works. Well, I've got no time for that
tomfoolery. I say that if you don't know something, you should
stand up and say so, not go round pretending you believe in
some mumbo-jumbo.

OSCAR

I can believe in anything, provided it's incredible. That's why
I intend to die a Catholic, though I couldn't possibly live as one.

QUEENSBERRY looks suspicious.

OSCAR *(cont.)*

Catholicism is such a romantic religion. It has saints and sinners.
The Church of England only has respectable people who believe
in respectability. You get to be a bishop, not by what you
believe, but by what you don't.

QUEENSBERRY

That's true enough!

OSCAR

It's the only church where the sceptic stands at the altar, and St
Thomas the doubter is prince of the apostles. No, I couldn't
possibly die in the Church of England.

QUEENSBERRY
Where do you stand on cremation?

OSCAR
I'm not sure I have a position.

QUEENSBERRY
I'm for it. I wrote a poem. 'When I am dead, cremate me', that's how it begins. 'When I am dead, cremate me.' What do you think of that for an opening line?

OSCAR
It's challenging.

QUEENSBERRY
Well, I'm a challenging sort of man. That's why people don't like me. I don't go along with the ordinary ways of thinking.

OSCAR
Then we are exactly alike.

QUEENSBERRY isn't sure about that.

OSCAR (cont.)
Another glass of brandy? I find that alcohol, taken in sufficient quantities, can produce all the effects of drunkenness.

54

EXTERIOR
Stables
1894. DAY

QUEENSBERRY is looking at horses, feeling their legs, watching as they're trotted up and down for him. BOSIE is with him. Both are trying to keep calm, but a fight is inevitable.

BOSIE
You were there for ages.

(he laughs)

                              BOSIE *(cont.)*
You stayed talking till after four. I knew you'd like him
once you'd met him.

                          QUEENSBERRY
Well – he's got charm, I admit that.

(he frowns)

          But that's bad. Men shouldn't be charming. Disgusting.

(to the Groom)

          I don't think much of his action. Let's have a look at the bay.

He turns back to BOSIE.

                      QUEENSBERRY *(cont.)*
Mind you, Wilde's no fool. Talks wonderfully,
really wonderfully.

(he frowns again)

          But that means nothing when what he says is such rot. Worse
          than rot. Evil. Which is why I insist you stop seeing him
          forthwith.

                              BOSIE
Insist? What's that supposed to mean?

                          QUEENSBERRY
It means I will cut off your allowance if you don't do as I say.

He watches the new horse.

                      QUEENSBERRY *(cont.)*

(to the Groom)

          Trot him up and down a bit.

He turns back to BOSIE.

                              BOSIE
          Look, father –

QUEENSBERRY *(cont.)*

You wasted your time at Oxford, pretending you were going into the Foreign Office – and thank God you didn't, when that Jew queer Rosebery can become Foreign Secretary and bugger all the juniors – including your brother –

BOSIE

That's all lies.

QUEENSBERRY

You spent your whole time writing obscene poetry!

BOSIE

My poems aren't obscene!

QUEENSBERRY

They're in the manner of Wilde. That's filthy enough for me.

He watches the horse.

BOSIE

Have you ever actually read any of Oscar's poems?

QUEENSBERRY

I wouldn't sully my mind with perverted trash like that.

(to Trainer)

Tell him to pick his feet up - he's not straight!

BOSIE

Are you calling Oscar a pervert? Because that's libellous!

QUEENSBERRY has his position worked out already.

QUEENSBERRY

I'm not saying he *is* one. I'm saying he's *posing* as one. Which is worse. His wife's divorcing him. Did you know that? For sodomy.

BOSIE

That's completely untrue!

QUEENSBERRY

I hope it is. Because if it *were* true, I'd shoot him on sight.

(He looks quite capable of it, too.)

QUEENSBERRY *(cont.)*

You will cease to see Wilde, or I will cut you off without a penny.

BOSIE is white with rage. But he controls himself.

BOSIE

As though I wanted your money. What little you have left from your tarts.

QUEENSBERRY

How dare you speak to your father like that!

BOSIE

What a funny little man you are.

He turns and goes.

QUEENSBERRY

Bosie! Come back here, you filthy-minded cissy!

BOSIE stops and shouts back at him.

BOSIE

You're absurd!

QUEENSBERRY is apoplectic.

QUEENSBERRY

And you're nothing but a bumboy!

BOSIE

You're pathetic!

QUEENSBERRY

Bosie!

But BOSIE has gone.

55

EXTERIOR

London Park

1894. DAY

PEOPLE are riding their horses. Not far from the Row, BOSIE is trying to twirl a silver revolver in a professional gun-slinger's manner, but he's not very good. He has a dangerous glint in his eye, he is reckless, laughing, happy. He looks like his father. OSCAR is looking very apprehensive, as are the BYSTANDERS.

> BOSIE
> I'm a bloody good shot, better than he is! I'll shoot him through the heart, if he threatens me!

> OSCAR
> Hadn't you better use a silver bullet then?

BOSIE fires at a passing pigeon. The bullet splinters the branches of a tree. A horse bolts. There is considerable public indignation.

> BOSIE
> There's one for the Black Douglas!

> OSCAR
> Bosie, for God's sake –

BOSIE fires off more shots, laughing like a madman.

> BOSIE
> And one for his liver and one for his lights and one for his stinking rotten soul!

Cowering as the bullets go in all directions, OSCAR looks at BOSIE almost with pity. Now the gun is empty, BOSIE suddenly becomes frightened at himself.

OSCAR
Bosie!

BOSIE
I'll save one for myself. My own *father*. He wants to kill me.

56

INTERIOR

London Hotel

SUITE. 1894. DAY

OSCAR has BOSIE's head on his shoulder.

OSCAR
My life is everything I ever wanted. I have fame. I have recognition. With two plays about to open in London, I may even have money. The world is at my command. Yet I can't command myself. I can't command my feelings for you.

57

EXTERIOR

London Hotel

1894. DAY

CONSTANCE arrives in a cab. A FOOTMAN runs up and opens the door.

58

INTERIOR

London Hotel

SUITE. 1894. DAY

OSCAR and BOSIE are having breakfast in the sitting-room. They are half-dressed, in dressing-gowns. OSCAR is answering the door.

He finds CONSTANCE, but is only momentarily surprised. He kisses her on the cheek. BOSIE rises, all confidence. He too kisses her, like an old friend.

> OSCAR
>
> Constance, my dear, how nice.

> BOSIE
>
> Constance!

> CONSTANCE
>
> Bosie –

(she turns to Oscar in confusion)

> I've brought you your letters. You haven't been home for so long –

> OSCAR
>
> Thank you.

> BOSIE
>
> It's so much more convenient for Oscar, living in the West End, when he has a play coming on.

> OSCAR
>
> Yes, I'm like one of those northern businessmen who has to keep an eye on his factory.

It falls very flat. BOSIE sees that CONSTANCE is almost in tears and is silent.

> CONSTANCE
>
> The boys ask for you all the time. They're longing to see you.

OSCAR feels ashamed.

> BOSIE
>
> Oscar has to make sure the play's a success, Constance.

> OSCAR
>
> I'll come round this afternoon. For tea.

> BOSIE
>
> It's the dress rehearsal this afternoon.

It's a challenge for mastery. CONSTANCE waits.

> OSCAR
>
> Tomorrow, then. I'll come tomorrow.

> CONSTANCE
>
> Tomorrow then.

> OSCAR
>
> Goodbye, my dear.

She goes over and kisses OSCAR and goes to the door. BOSIE springs up to open it for her.

> CONSTANCE
>
> Goodbye.

> BOSIE
>
> Goodbye Constance.

CONSTANCE goes.

59

EXTERIOR

Worthing Pier

1894. DAY

OSCAR, CYRIL and VYVYAN are fishing from the pier. OSCAR baiting the hooks for his BOYS, while CONSTANCE watches under a parasol with the NANNY. They seem a very happy family group. OSCAR sneezes.

> CONSTANCE
>
> I think I'd better stay. You're getting a cold.
>
> OSCAR
>
> No, no, I'm all right. Let's get the boys some ices. Boys, you've got to stay and look after Nanny.
>
> CONSTANCE
>
> I can take the boys to the dentist on Thursday, on their way back to boarding school.
>
> OSCAR
>
> Ah, but the whole point of them having dentistry now is so that they can stuff themselves with sweets for a whole week before we lose them.

OSCAR sneezes again.

> CONSTANCE
>
> Are you quite sure?
>
> OSCAR
>
> Bosie'll look after me.

60

EXTERIOR

Worthing

ANOTHER PART OF THE PIER. 1894. DAY

YOUNG MEN are bathing naked off the end of the pier. BOSIE is watching the YOUNG MEN disport themselves with keen interest.

61

INTERIOR

Worthing

LODGINGS. 1894. NIGHT

OSCAR is in bed with flu, feeling sorry for himself, and resentful that BOSIE has abandoned him. We hear the front door slam below and BOSIE come running upstairs.

BOSIE(o/s)

Oscar! Get your coat on – quick! I've got a present for you!

He appears, flushed with drink.

BOSIE*(cont.)*

Oh, God, you're not still seedy, are you?

OSCAR

Bosie, where have you *been*? I've had no one to talk to, no one to look after me –

BOSIE

Don't be so pathetic. I've found you the divinest boy!

OSCAR

Bosie, you promised Constance –

BOSIE

Bugger Constance! I'm not your Nanny! Come on, we're going out!

He is furious at having his plans for the evening thwarted.

OSCAR

Bosie - please ...

BOSIE

You look such an idiot lying there. Revolting. Have you forgotten how to wash?

OSCAR

As a matter of fact I'm dying for a glass of water.

BOSIE

Well, help yourself. You know where the jug is.

OSCAR

Bosie, darling –

BOSIE

It *stinks* in here. You'll be wanting me to empty your chamber-pot next.

He moves into the next room.

OSCAR

I emptied your chamber-pot. I looked after you.

BOSIE comes flashing back in.

BOSIE

Well, I'm not looking after you. Not now. You don't interest me, not when you're ill. You're just a boring middle-aged man with a blocked-up nose.

OSCAR

Bosie – dearest boy –

BOSIE

Shut up! Dearest boy, darling Bosie – it doesn't mean anything! You don't love me. The only person you've ever loved is yourself. You *like* me, you lust after me, you go about with me, because I've got a title, that's all. You like to write about dukes and duchesses, but you know nothing about them. You're the biggest snob I've ever met. And you think you're so daring because you fuck the occasional boy!

This is unbearable for OSCAR.

OSCAR

Bosie, please – you're killing me –

BOSIE

You'll just about do when you're at your best, you're *amusing*, very *amusing*, but when you're not at your best, you're no one.

He starts towards the door.

OSCAR

All I asked for was a glass of water.

BOSIE explodes.

BOSIE

For Christ's sake! There you are, then!

He throws the jug at OSCAR. He seems quite mad.

BOSIE *(cont.)*

Now will you shut up about the fucking water!

OSCAR is genuinely frightened of him now.

BOSIE *(cont.)*

There are two boys waiting out there. If you're not coming, I'll fuck them both myself. I'll take them to the Grand and fuck them in front of the whole fucking hotel. Then I'll send you the bill.

He goes. OSCAR lies there, knowing it will always be like this with BOSIE.

62

INTERIOR

Tite Street

DRAWING ROOM. 1894. DAY

A lighted match held under a brandy glass to warm it. ROSS hands the drink to OSCAR.

ROSS

Drink this. It will help your fever.

OSCAR still looks under the weather, and is well wrapped up. ROBBIE helps himself to a drink.

OSCAR

He's ashamed of loving men. His father bullies him – his mother spoils him and then berates him for being spoiled – neither of them gives him any real love. They're torturing him. And what's truly dreadful is that – when he can't bear it, and – he has one of his – he becomes exactly like his father. And he hates himself for that.

ROSS

You're too kind about him, Oscar.

OSCAR

You can't be too kind about someone who's been so – so hurt. Yet – if I go on trying to come between Bosie and his father – they'll destroy me.

ROSS

Bosie's quite capable of destroying you on his own. Look how much you wrote while he was away. Two wonderful plays which will run for years – back comes Bosie – what have you written since?

OSCAR *doesn't like to admit this.*

ROSS*(cont.)*

Oscar – you know how much I love and admire you – but you're throwing your genius away – for what?

OSCAR *is quite bitter.*

OSCAR

It's highly ironic. Queensberry thinks Bosie and I are locked in nightly embrace, when in reality we've been the purest model of Greek love since –

ROSS *is intrigued.*

OSCAR*(cont.)*

Bosie doesn't like doing it with me. I've loved him, I've educated him –

ROSS

But he's never grown up. And he never will.

OSCAR has made up his mind.

OSCAR

I'm not taking him back, Robbie. Not again. I can't.

ROSS smiles, but OSCAR is very sad.

OSCAR *(cont.)*

I've been very foolish, and very fond, and now – I must grow up myself.

ROSS

Oh, please don't do that. You're an artist. Artists are always children at heart.

OSCAR gives him a smile of genuine gratitude.

OSCAR

Ah, Robbie, I sometimes wonder …?

ARTHUR comes in with a newspaper under his arm. He bends down and whispers in OSCAR's ear. He gives him the newspaper and leaves. OSCAR opens it and reads rapidly. He is horror-struck.

OSCAR

My God! Francis Douglas!

ROSS

What?

OSCAR

Bosie's brother! He's been found shot! He's dead.

OSCAR hands him the paper. ROSS snatches it up.

ROSS

But he's just got engaged, he …

OSCAR

Bosie! Oh, poor, poor Bosie! He'll be utterly distraught!

OSCAR gets up and leaves.

63

INTERIOR

Lady Queensberry's Drawing Room

1894. DAY

BOSIE is white-faced and weeping, but already grief is turning to anger. OSCAR is holding him, cradling him.

> BOSIE
> He killed himself. It was my father. He drove him to it.

> OSCAR
> I'm sure your father's just as upset as everyone else.

> BOSIE
> No, he's not. He says it's a judgement on Rosebery. And my mother. And me and you.

OSCAR can't answer that.

> BOSIE *(cont.)*
> We've got to stop him, Oscar. Before he drives my whole family to suicide.

> OSCAR
> Bosie, Bosie – I promise you – I won't let him hurt you ever again. I promise.

> BOSIE
> That's not enough. I want him stopped. I want the whole world to know what he's done … what an evil man he is.

64

INTERIOR

Café Royal

1894. NIGHT

*QUEENSBERRY barges into the restaurant and stares belligerently around. The HEAD
WAITER comes up to him.*

HEAD WAITER
Table, my lord?

QUEENSBERRY
Is Lord Alfred here? And that shit and sod Wilde?

The HEAD WAITER is taken aback.

HEAD WAITER
No, my lord, not tonight.

QUEENSBERRY
Bugger must be at Kettner's.

65

INTERIOR

London Hotel

RECEPTION. 1894. NIGHT

SAME NIGHT.
QUEENSBERRY comes barging into the hotel and up to the desk.

QUEENSBERRY
Is my son staying here?

The MANAGER looks at him blankly.

QUEENSBERRY *(cont.)*
Is Lord Alfred Douglas staying here?

MANAGER
No, sir, he is not.

QUEENSBERRY
What about Wilde?

MANAGER
No, sir.

QUEENSBERRY
If I find they have been staying here, I'll give you the biggest whipping of your life!

66

INTERIOR

London Hotel

SUITE. 1894. NIGHT

SAME NIGHT.

BOSIE is in bed with WOOD. In the background we see them fucking. OSCAR is smoking and watching. Champagne and glasses are on the table. After a few moments BOSIE climaxes. He rolls off. WOOD pulls the covers over them.

OSCAR
Well, I expect you two would like a drink after your exertions.

He starts to pour champagne. None of them hears the passkey being used in the sitting-room. The HOTEL MANAGER appears with a FLOOR WAITER looking excitedly over his shoulder. OSCAR turns. The MANAGER takes in the scene at a glance.

MANAGER

I must ask you to leave, Mr Wilde.

OSCAR is shaken and embarrassed, but keeps his cool.

OSCAR

My dear man, what are you talking about?

MANAGER

At once, please.

BOSIE

What's the matter? My father cracking the whip downstairs, is he?

The MANAGER gives WOOD a curt nod to tell him to get out, which WOOD rapidly does. BOSIE stays where he is.

MANAGER

My lord –

OSCAR

Bosie –

BOSIE

You're not frightened of what this little man thinks, are you?

OSCAR

I think – the pleasures of the evening should be resumed elsewhere.

BOSIE gets up and starts to dress, angry with OSCAR.

BOSIE

You're such a coward. You say you despise convention, but you're the most conventional man I know. Come on, then! If we're going, let's go!

He walks out, still half-dressed. The MANAGER holds the door for OSCAR.

67

EXTERIOR

Haymarket Theatre

1894. DAY

OSCAR comes out, saying goodbye to the STAGE DOORKEEPER.

OSCAR

Until tomorrow, Tommy!

DOORKEEPER

Goodbye, sir.

CHARLES PARKER and ALFRED WOOD step out of the shadows.

WOOD

Oscar! Wait a minute, Oscar!

OSCAR sees PARKER and WOOD and at once guesses there is going to be an attempt at blackmail. He is geniality itself.

OSCAR

Alfred! How nice to see you. And Charlie, looking so well. I'm afraid I'm busy this evening. But we must have dinner again soon.

WOOD

It's not a question of dinner. I've got a letter of yours. To Lord Alfred.

He shows OSCAR the letter, but keeps it out of reach.

PARKER

Nice letter, Oscar, beautiful. 'Lips like roses.
The madness of kisses in ancient Greece'.

OSCAR

Oh, then, I expect it's one of my prose poems.

This is not at all what they are expecting. But WOOD persists.

WOOD

There's a gentleman's offered me sixty pounds for it.

OSCAR

Then you must accept, Alfred. I've never received so large a sum for a prose work of that length in all my life. Tell your friend I'm delighted that someone in England values my work so highly.

WOOD

Well – he's gone away.

PARKER

He's gone to the country.

OSCAR

Well, I'm sure he'll be back soon.

OSCAR strolls on. WOOD and PARKER look at each other, then chase after him.

WOOD

Oscar! Oscar! Look, you couldn't let us have something – could you? I'm a bit short at the moment, and – you know –

OSCAR

Of course, of course. Here's half a sovereign. Now mind you take good care of that letter. Lord Alfred is going to publish it in sonnet form in his new magazine.

He saunters off. The BOYS look at one another again.

PARKER

For fuck's sake!

WOOD goes after OSCAR.

WOOD

Oscar!

OSCAR pauses. WOOD offers him the letter.

WOOD *(cont.)*

It's no good trying to rent you, you just laugh at us. Here.

OSCAR

Thank you.

He looks at the letter. It is very grubby.

WOOD
He can be very careless, Lord Alfred.

OSCAR
What a wonderfully wicked life you lead!

He saunters off.

OSCAR *(cont.)*
You boys! You boys!

68

INTERIOR

Tite Street

DINING-ROOM. 1894. NIGHT

OSCAR is dining alone. We hear the front door opening, then sounds of commotion coming from the hallway.

QUEENSBERRY (O/S)
Where is he?

ARTHUR (O/S)
Mr Wilde is not receiving any visitors.

QUEENSBERRY (O/S)
Where is he?

ARTHUR (O/S)
He's busy, sir.

ARTHUR comes in looking fraught.

ARTHUR
Excuse me, sir, there's a gentleman –

QUEENSBERRY, accompanied by a gnarled and cauliflower-eared BOXER, thrusts ARTHUR aside.

QUEENSBERRY

You! Listen to me!

OSCAR *rises.*

QUEENSBERRY *(cont.)*

You're a bugger!

OSCAR

I don't allow people to talk to me like that in my own house, Lord Queensberry. Or anywhere else. I suppose you've come to apologize for the lies that you've been spreading about me?

QUEENSBERRY

I've come to tell you to leave my son alone! You sodomite!

OSCAR *turns to the BOXER.*

OSCAR

The Marquess appears to be obsessed with other people's sexual activities. Has it anything to do with his new wife, I wonder? And the fact she's seeking divorce for non-consummation?

The BOXER is too flabbergasted to speak. QUEENSBERRY is white with anger.

QUEENSBERRY

Unless you swear that you'll have nothing more to do with Bosie, I shall go to Scotland Yard!

OSCAR

You can go to the devil! You and your – who is this gargoyle?

He means the BOXER, who looks menacingly back.

QUEENSBERRY

You're a queer and a – sham! A poseur! If I catch you and Bosie together again I'll give you such a thrashing –

OSCAR *turns again to the BOXER.*

OSCAR

I believe Lord Queensberry once invented some Rules for boxing. I've no idea what they are. But the Oscar Wilde rule is to shoot on sight. Now kindly leave my house.

QUEENSBERRY

You can shut up! I shall leave when I'm damn well ready.

He raises his whip in menacing fashion. OSCAR strides up to QUEENSBERRY, grabs the whip from him, and snaps it in two. QUEENSBERRY is somewhat taken aback.

QUEENSBERRY *(cont.)*

It's a scandal, what you've been doing!

OSCAR

All the scandal is your own. Your treatment of your wives. Your neglect of your children. And above all, the depraved insistence that they be as tyrannical and unloving as you are yourself.

He turns to ARTHUR.

OSCAR *(cont.)*

Arthur, this is the Marquess of Queensberry, the most infamous brute and the least tender father in London. Never let him into my house again.

ARTHUR opens the door. QUEENSBERRY doesn't know how to go with dignity. He nods to the BOXER.

QUEENSBERRY

Very well, then. Let's get out of this — stew.

They go. When he is alone, OSCAR allows his mask of cool control to slip. We see he is trembling — with anger, as well as fear.

69

INTERIOR

St James's Theatre

1895. NIGHT

An eager CROWD take their seats for the opening night of The Importance of Being Ernest. *Green carnations are sported in all the YOUNG MEN's buttonholes and on the dresses of Oscar's WOMEN FRIENDS. We see ADA arriving, and SPERANZA, CONSTANCE, GRAY, ROSS, BOSIE, LADY MOUNT-TEMPLE etc.*

70

EXTERIOR

St James's Theatre

STAGE DOOR. 1895. NIGHT

There is a scuffle as TWO POLICEMEN wrestle with QUEENSBERRY and the BOXER. QUEENSBERRY is shouting obscenities. Finally the POLICEMEN push them away from the stage door. QUEENSBERRY grabs a small bundle from the BOXER. He throws its contents – raw vegetables – at the OFFICERS.

QUEENSBERRY

I want you to give that to Oscar Wilde.

POLICEMAN

Thank you, sir, we'll take care of it.

QUEENSBERRY

I wanted to give it to him personally. As a bouquet.

POLICEMAN

I dare say you did, sir, but you're not going to.

Thwarted, QUEENSBERRY turns away, frowning angrily.
QUEENSBERRY
Cur! Sod and a bugger! You remember that!

71

INTERIOR

St James's Theatre

1895. NIGHT

It is the end of the play. We come in on a huge roar of laughter. JACK has the Army List. He puts it down and speaks quite calmly to GWENDOLEN.
JACK
I always told you, Gwendolen, my name was Ernest, didn't I? Well, it is Ernest after all. I mean, it naturally is Ernest.

Laugh.

LADY BRACKNELL
Yes, I remember now that the General was called Ernest. I knew I had some particular reason for disliking the name.

Laugh. ADA thinks the whole thing very funny, but LADY MOUNT-TEMPLE has recognized herself and is not at all amused.
GWENDOLEN
Ernest! My own Ernest! I knew from the first you could have had no other name!

JACK
Gwendolen, it is a terrible thing for a man to find out suddenly that all his life he has been speaking nothing but the truth. Can you forgive me?

GWENDOLEN
I can. For I feel you are sure to change.

Laugh.

JACK

My own one!

CHASUBLE

Laetitia!

MISS PRISM

Frederick! At last!

We observe OSCAR watching the end of the play from the wings.

ALGERNON

Cecily! At last!

JACK

Gwendolen! At last!

All THREE COUPLES are now embracing one another.

LADY BRACKNELL

My nephew, you seem to be displaying signs of triviality.

JACK

On the contrary, Aunt Augusta, I've now realized for the first
time in my life the vital Importance of Being Ernest.

*The curtain falls. There is a storm of applause, a standing ovation. GEORGE
ALEXANDER, the actor-manager, comes to lead OSCAR on. OSCAR puts out his
cigarette and goes out on stage.*

*The applause is enormous as he takes his bow. We see the audience from OSCAR's point of
view. We see his FRIENDS, laughing and clapping. It is the best moment of his life.*

72

EXTERIOR
Albemarle Club
1895. DAY

The MEMBERS go their ways as OSCAR goes in.

PORTER

Mr Wilde, sir.

OSCAR

Yes?

The PORTER hands him an envelope.

OSCAR

Thank you.

OSCAR takes out a card. He frowns as he tries to read it. Then realization dawns. He is appalled.

73

INTERIOR
Cadogan Hotel
SUITE. 1895. DAY

OSCAR is with BOSIE, who is highly excited, and ROSS, who is trying to read the card.

ROSS

To Oscar Wilde – ponce, is it? Ponce and – sodomite?

BOSIE

'Posing as a sodomite.' He's illiterate. Illiterate, ignorant –

OSCAR

It's hideous.

BOSIE

We've got him now, Robbie! He wrote it down, the porter read it. That makes it a public libel. Now we can take him to court.

ROSS is appalled and turns to OSCAR.

ROSS

For God's sake, Oscar – Oscar, you mustn't do that, that would be – I mean –

BOSIE

We've just been waiting for a chance to get him in the dock and show the world what a swine and shit he's always been. To me, my mother, my brothers –

ROSS

But he'll plead justification. He'll call all the renters as witnesses for the defence.

BOSIE

Of course he won't. He doesn't know what a renter is.

ROSS

No? I hear he's had detectives following you ever since you came back from Egypt.

BOSIE

He can't prove anything. But we can. We can prove he's the vilest man that ever walked the earth.

ROSS sees he'll get nowhere arguing with BOSIE and turns to OSCAR.

ROSS

Tear the card up, Oscar. Pretend you never got it.

BOSIE quickly takes the card to protect it.

BOSIE

Are you mad? That's our main piece of evidence!

> ROSS
> I'm sure, if Oscar went abroad for a few months, lived on his royalties while your father calms down –

> BOSIE
> Whose side are you on?

> ROSS
> Bosie, if this goes to court, Oscar will have to tell lies. Perjure himself. Everything will come out. Whatever the result – it'll be utter disaster.

> BOSIE
> You're an enemy, then!

> OSCAR
> No, no – Bosie – please. Robbie, you're a dear boy, but I can't even think of leaving the country. As a matter of fact I can't even leave this hotel.

ROSS *stares at him.*

> OSCAR *(cont.)*
> I can't pay the bill.

> ROSS
> We can raise you money, for heaven's sake. Anyway, what about your royalties?

> BOSIE
> We shall need all the money we can get for the libel case.

ROSS *is furious, but restrains himself.*

> BOSIE *(cont.)*
> My father can't go on making all our lives a torment like this.

> ROSS
> Oscar, I beg you –

> OSCAR
> I'm not going to run away, Robbie. I'm not going to hide. That would be the English thing to do.

ROSS
If you take Queensberry to court, all hell will break loose.

OSCAR
All my life I've fought against the English vice.

ROSS and BOSIE both look startled. OSCAR smiles.

OSCAR *(cont.)*
Hypocrisy.

There is nothing lofty about this. It's a statement of fact, an acceptance of doom.

OSCAR *(cont.)*
Not that that's the point. The point is, Queensberry's already caused the death of one of his sons. If I don't try and stop him now – who will he harm next?

ROSS sees it is hopeless.

74

INTERIOR

Tite Street

DRAWING ROOM. 1895. DAY

ROSS is with CONSTANCE, who is walking up and down to ease her painful back. They are both embarrassed.

CONSTANCE
He's avoiding me, Robbie.

She looks at him. He looks away.

CONSTANCE
I know what everyone's saying, but it's not true. It's not true, is it?

ROSS
Of course not.

But she doesn't know whether to believe him or not.

CONSTANCE

It's so shaming.

She leans on a chair in pain, ROSS jumps up to help her sit.

CONSTANCE*(cont.)*

No, I – I find it easier to stand. I'm going to Torquay for a month, to try and get my back right. Oscar's been so busy –

ROSS

I'm sure he'll be terribly upset when he knows you've been in so much pain.

She waves that aside.

CONSTANCE

The truth is, I need some money. I'm not even sure where he is to ask for it.

ROSS is shocked.

CONSTANCE*(cont.)*

It does seem rather hard when he's having such an extraordinary success ...

ROSS's loyalty is divided.

ROSS

I think I can find him.

ROSS is silent. CONSTANCE goes to sit. ROSS helps her now.

CONSTANCE*(cont.)*

I keep hearing these stories about Bosie and his father.

ROSS

I'm sure you don't want to –

CONSTANCE

Oh yes, I do. Men think women should be protected by not knowing. Not knowing only makes it worse. Is there going to be trouble?

ROSS

I hope not.

75

Humphreys' Office

1895. DAY

C.O. HUMPHREYS is a bald solicitor of no great acumen. The room is bleak. BOSIE and OSCAR are with him. BOSIE is still highly excited.

HUMPHREYS
I believe a prosecution would certainly succeed, provided, and I stress this, provided there is no truth whatever in the accusation made by Lord Queensberry.

BOSIE
Of course there's no truth in it!

OSCAR seems unperturbed. Fate is taking its course.

HUMPHREYS
Then so long as I have Mr Wilde's assurance that that is indeed the case ...

Silence. HUMPHREYS waits uncomfortably for OSCAR to respond. The silence continues. Then OSCAR looks up.

OSCAR
There is no truth in the accusation whatever.

HUMPHREYS
Good. Excellent. The defence, I understand, will be led by Mr Edward Carson.

OSCAR
Old Ned? I was at college with him in Dublin. No doubt he will perform his task with all the added bitterness of an old friend.

76

Courtroom

1895. DAY

The court is crowded, not a seat to be had. QUEENSBERRY is wearing a Cambridge blue hunting stock instead of a collar and tie. OSCAR is dressed in the height of fashion, with a buttonhole. He is being cross-examined by EDWARD CARSON, a tall, saturnine man with a rich Irish accent.

> OSCAR
>
> In writing a book or play, I'm concerned entirely with literature – with art. I do not aim at doing good or evil, but at making a thing that will have some quality of beauty.
>
> CARSON
>
> Well, listen sir – here is one of your pieces of literature: 'Wickedness is a myth invented by good people to account for the curious attractiveness of others.'

There is amusement in court.

> CARSON *(cont.)*
>
> D'you think that true?
>
> OSCAR
>
> I rarely think anything I write is true.
>
> CARSON
>
> 'If one tells the truth, one is sure, sooner or later, to be found out'?
>
> OSCAR
>
> That is a pleasing paradox, but I do not set very high store by it as an axiom.

CARSON
Is it good for the young?

OSCAR
Anything is good that stimulates thought at whatever age.

CARSON
Whether moral or immoral?

OSCAR
There is no such thing as morality or immorality in thought.

CARSON
Well, what about this, then? 'Pleasure is the only thing one should live for'?

OSCAR
I think that the realization of oneself is the prime aim of life, and that to realize through pleasure is finer than to do so through pain. I am, on this point, entirely on the side of the ancients – the Greeks.

He is completely self-assured. SUPPORTERS in the gallery laugh.

77

INTERIOR

Court

CORRIDOR. 1895. DAY

Many of the BOYS that OSCAR has frequented are waiting to give evidence, including TAYLOR, WOOD, ALLEN and PARKER. They are smoking and joking.

CARSON(o/s)
How long have you known Alfred Taylor?

OSCAR(o/s)
About two years, two and a half years.

78

INTERIOR

Courtroom

1895. DAY

OSCAR is less confident now, and the subject has changed from literature to life.

CARSON

Is he an intimate friend of yours?

OSCAR

Well, I wouldn't call him that. No.

CARSON

But you went often to his rooms.

OSCAR

About seven or eight times, perhaps.

CARSON

Did you know Mr Taylor kept ladies' dresses in his rooms?

OSCAR

No.

The courtroom is very tense. QUEENSBERRY is looking pleased.

CARSON

Did you know he was notorious for introducing young men to older men?

OSCAR

I – I never heard it in my life.

CARSON

Has he introduced young men to you?

OSCAR

Yes.

                    CARSON
How many young men?

                    OSCAR
About five.

                    CARSON
What were their occupations?

                    OSCAR
I really don't know.

                    CARSON
Oh, well let me tell you, Mr Wilde. You met a man called
Charles Parker there, I believe.

                    OSCAR
Yes.

                    CARSON
Charles Parker is a gentleman's valet.

He lets this sink in. The faces of the JURY tell us OSCAR has lost the case.

                    CARSON *(cont.)*
You met his brother there, too, I believe.

                    OSCAR
Yes.

                    CARSON
He is a groom.

Again, he leaves a pause. Again the faces of the JURY show us OSCAR is doomed.

                    OSCAR
I didn't care tuppence what they were. I liked them. I have a
passion to civilize the community. I recognize no social
distinctions at all, of any kind. To me youth, the mere fact of
youth, is so wonderful that I would sooner talk to a young man
for half an hour than – well, than to be cross-examined in
Court.

CARSON

So, do I understand that even a young boy you might pick up in the street would be a pleasing companion?

OSCAR

I would talk to a street arab with pleasure. If he would talk to me.

CARSON

And take him to your rooms?

OSCAR

Yes.

CARSON

And then commit improprieties with him?

The question seems to come out of nowhere. It rocks OSCAR.

OSCAR

Certainly not. Certainly not.

No one in court believes him.

79

INTERIOR

Humphreys' Office

1895. DAY

HUMPHREYS is looking very grave. OSCAR is with him.

HUMPHREYS

You withdraw your libel action against Lord Queensberry – well and good. But there remains the question of the evidence, Lord Queensberry's evidence against you. My information is that the Crown wishes to pursue the matter. In which case an arrest and a charge of gross indecency are certain to follow. The maximum sentence is two years hard labour.

OSCAR doesn't know what to say or do.

HUMPHREYS(cont.)

Nine months hard labour is reckoned to be more than a man of our background can survive.

OSCAR

But the children, the boys – I must go and see them, I –

HUMPHREYS

You have no time for that.

OSCAR can't grasp it yet.

OSCAR

But, but – my wife. I have to say goodbye to my wife.

HUMPHREYS

Unless you positively wish to subject her to the further humiliation of seeing you arrested and taken away in front of the gutter press, Mr Wilde, you must *go*.

<h1 style="text-align:center">80</h1>

EXTERIOR

<h1 style="text-align:center">Cadogan Hotel</h1>

1895. DAY

The gutter PRESS is out in force outside the Cadogan Hotel, clamouring to be let in along with a crowd of eager SPECTATORS.

81

INTERIOR

Cadogan Hotel Suite

1895. DAY

OSCAR looks stunned. BOSIE goes to refill OSCAR's glass of hock and seltzer. BOSIE has one already for himself. ROSS is coming in.

ROSS

Oscar, you must take that train. Practically everyone you know will be on it. At least six hundred single gentlemen, all in abject terror of arrest.

OSCAR

No. Where your life leads you, you must go. I defy society.

82

INTERIOR

Tite Street

DRAWING ROOM. 1895. DAY

ROSS is with CONSTANCE.

CONSTANCE

Tell him to go. He must save himself. Tell him to go abroad.

ROSS

We've been telling him all day. He won't budge.

She nods, expecting it.

CONSTANCE

People have never understood the courage he needed to be himself.

ROSS waits a moment.

ROSS

You must go abroad too.

She takes a moment to comprehend the full significance of this.

ROSS *(cont.)*

We must *all* go abroad. At once.

Silence.

ROSS *(cont.)*

Oscar says – will you tell the boys goodbye?

She nods, bitter.

ROSS *(cont.)*

I need to go through his papers.

CONSTANCE

I was always too silent. If I'd known – Bosie – if I'd only spoken up.

ROSS

It wouldn't have made any difference.

CONSTANCE

Perhaps not. But at least I wouldn't blame myself now.

83

INTERIOR

Tite Street

STUDY. 1895. DAY

ROSS is going rapidly through papers, removing manuscripts, destroying letters. He comes on a cache of photographs: here are WOOD, TAYLOR and PARKER. ROSS quickly puts them in a case.

84

INTERIOR

Cadogan Hotel Suite

BEDROOM. 1895. DAY

SPERANZA is at her most exalted. OSCAR is utterly downcast.

SPERANZA

You are an Irish gentleman. Of course you must stay.

OSCAR just looks at her.

SPERANZA *(cont.)*

Your father fought when he was libelled. I was in the courts myself, I fought.

OSCAR

Yes, I know Madre.

BOSIE and ROSS wait in the sitting-room smoking cigarettes.

SPERANZA

You will fight these English philistines and you will win! And even if you lose – if you go to prison – you will always be my son.

OSCAR

Well, of course, it's too late to change that now.

The joke does not go down well.

SPERANZA

If you go, Oscar, I will never speak to you again.

OSCAR

No one will ever speak to me again whatever I do.

(he is serious)

Of course I am your son, Madre. Which is why – even if I lose – the English will never forget me.

He is telling her he loves her. She throws her arms round him.

85

INTERIOR

Cadogan Hotel

CORRIDOR. 1895. DAY

SPERANZA with great dignity leaves the suite. She finds a chair in the corridor and sits. She lets the mask slip and breaks down, sobbing.

86

EXTERIOR

Cadogan Hotel

1895. DAY

Head held high, SPERANZA comes out of the hotel to where the PORTER has got her a cab. She gets into the cab. One or two REPORTERS chase after it.

REPORTER

Lady Wilde! Lady Wilde! Have you anything to say about your son's disgrace? Lady Wilde? Have you anything to say?

87

INTERIOR

Cadogan Hotel Suite

1895. EVENING

OSCAR is sitting with ROSS when the knock comes. He looks stunned. They look at each other. There comes a second, more peremptory knock.

ROSS

Come in.

TWO DETECTIVES appear.

DETECTIVE 1

Mr Wilde, I believe?

ROSS

Yes. Yes.

DETECTIVE 1

We have a warrant here for your arrest, on a charge of committing indecent acts.

88

EXTERIOR

St. James's Theatre

1895. DAY

OSCAR's name is being blacked out on the posters for The Importance of Being Earnest.

89

EXTERIOR

Savoy Theatre

1895. DAY

'Last performances' stickers are going up for An Ideal Husband.

90

INTERIOR

Tite Street

DRAWING ROOM. DAY

Most of the paintings have been taken down. Some of the furniture is covered in dust sheets. Large packing cases are visible. ADA and LADY MOUNT-TEMPLE are in their coats and hats. LADY MOUNT-TEMPLE is in full flight. CONSTANCE is weathering the storm. ADA is watching and listening.

LADY MOUNT-TEMPLE

I recommend Switzerland. As soon as possible. You will have to change your name, of course.

CONSTANCE

Oh, I can't –

LADY MOUNT-TEMPLE

My dear Constance, the name of 'Wilde' will be a word of execration for the next thousand years. You can't possibly let your boys grow up with people knowing who they are. Think of their lives at school.

CONSTANCE is shaken, but has had enough.

CONSTANCE

Thank you for your advice. I'm sorry our friendship has to end like this.

LADY MOUNT-TEMPLE

You will always be my friend.

CONSTANCE

I'm still Oscar's wife.

LADY MOUNT-TEMPLE is very severe.

LADY MOUNT-TEMPLE

That must cease forthwith. Forthwith, do you understand? Anyone who has anything to do with Oscar from now on will never be received in society again. Ever.

She goes. CONSTANCE moves away, fighting the tears. ADA comes to comfort her.

CONSTANCE

Oh God, Ada, what is going to happen to him?

91

INTERIOR

Holloway Prison

CORRIDOR

TWO PRISON OFFICERS watch BOSIE walking downstairs.

PRISON OFFICER
That's Oscar Wilde's boy.

92

INTERIOR

Holloway Prison

INTERVIEW ROOM. 1895. DAY

BOSIE is talking to OSCAR through a grille. Other PRISONERS are talking to their FRIENDS, and there are OFFICERS everywhere. OSCAR is very downcast. BOSIE is very wild.

BOSIE
Oscar, you must let me go in the witness box. If the jury can only hear what I have to say –

OSCAR
Bosie – darling boy – As soon as they see you in all your golden youth and me in all my – corruption –

He has never spoken to BOSIE of his physical self-disgust before.

BOSIE
You didn't corrupt me! I corrupted you, if anything!

> OSCAR

That's not how it will seem.

> BOSIE

But I must have my say! It's outrageous, everyone else has said everything, anything that came into his head, but I'm the person all this is about! It's *me* my father wants to get at, not you! It's outrageous that I can't have my say!

> OSCAR

It won't help, Bosie. It may actually make things worse.

> BOSIE

But my father will win! I can't endure my father winning!

And that is true; it is against his father, not for Oscar, that he wants to give evidence.

> OSCAR

You must go away, dear boy. I couldn't bear for them to arrest *you*.

> BOSIE

I can't bear what they're saying about you in court!

A bell rings.

> BOSIE *(cont.)*

Jesus Christ!

BOSIE rises.

> OSCAR

Goodbye Bosie, dear boy.

OSCAR takes his fingers through the grille and kisses them.

> OSCAR *(cont.)*

Don't let anyone, anything, ever change your feeling for me. Change your love.

> BOSIE

Oscar, never! They never will. I won't let them. I won't let them.

BOSIE has to go. OSCAR watches him go. We hear GILL in voice-over.

93

Courtroom

OSCAR is being questioned by CHARLES GILL for the Prosecution. QUEENSBERRY is listening, wearing a white cravat and a flower.

GILL

You have been a great deal in the company of Lord Alfred Douglas.

OSCAR

Oh, yes.

GILL

Did he read his poems to you?

OSCAR

Yes.

GILL

So, you can perhaps understand that some of his verses would not be acceptable to a reader with an ordinary balanced mind?

OSCAR

I am not prepared to say. It is a question of taste, temperament and individuality. I should say that one man's poetry is another man's poison.

GILL

Yes, I daresay. But in this poem by Lord Alfred Douglas – *Two Loves* – there is one love – 'True Love' – which, and I quote, 'fills the hearts of boy and girl with mutual flame'. And there is another – 'I am the love that dare not speak its name'. Was that poem explained to you?

OSCAR

I think it is clear.

GILL

There is no question as to what it means?

OSCAR

Most certainly not.

GILL

Is it not clear that the love described relates to natural and unnatural love?

OSCAR

No.

GILL

Oh. Then what is the 'Love that dare not speak its name'?

OSCAR

'The love that dare not speak its name' in this century is such a great affection of an elder for a younger man as there was between David and Jonathan, such as Plato made the very basis of his philosophy and such as you may find in the sonnets of Michelangelo and Shakespeare. It is in this century misunderstood, so much misunderstood that it may be described as 'the Love that dare not speak its name', and on account of it I am placed where I am now. It is beautiful, it is fine, it is the noblest form of affection. There is nothing unnatural about it. It is intellectual, and it repeatedly exists between an elder and a younger man, when the elder has intellect, and the younger man has all the joy, hope and glamour of life before him. That it should be so, the world does not understand. The world mocks at it and sometimes puts one in the pillory for it.

There is a spontaneous outburst of applause from the public gallery; but there are also hisses. The JUDGE raps with his mallet.

We hear the JUDGE giving sentence as we see OSCAR in the dock.

JUDGE(o/s)

Oscar Wilde, the crime of which you have been convicted is so bad that I shall pass the severest sentence that the law will allow. In my judgement it is totally inadquate for such a case as this. It is the worst case I have ever tried.

94

INTERIOR

Court Corridor

DAY

OSCAR is being marched down a corridor. It is crowded on both sides. PEOPLE jostle to get a view. There is jeering and shouting. A MAN spits at him. The JUDGE continues.

JUDGE(o/s)

The sentence of the court is that you will be imprisoned and held to hard labour for two years.

By the door, someone steps out from the CROWD and stands conspicuously apart, as OSCAR approaches. It is ROSS. As OSCAR comes past, ROSS raises his hat in a sign of loyalty. OSCAR sees this and the tears come to his eyes.

He is marched away downstairs. ROSS stares after him. The door closes.

95

INTERIOR

Holloway Prison Yard

1895. DAY

We see OSCAR among PRISONERS trudging round and round. He is hooded.
We hear OSCAR over.

OSCAR(o/s)

A slim thing, gold-haired like an angel, stands always
at my side. He moves in the gloom like a white flower.
I thought but to defend him from his father.
I thought of nothing else. Now – my life seems
to have gone from me. I am caught in a terrible
net. But so long as I think he is thinking of me –

We see OSCAR on the treadmill and in his cell.

OSCAR(o/s)

My sweet rose, my delicate flower, my lily of lilies,
it is in prison that I shall test the power of love.
I shall see if I can't make the bitter waters sweet by
the intensity of the love I bear you.

96

EXTERIOR

Italian Terrace and Garden

1897. DAY

BOSIE and ROSS are on the terrace. BOSIE is feeling very sorry for himself.

BOSIE

He *asked* me not to change. Those were his last words to me:
Don't change.

ROSS

Well, things are going to have to change when he comes out.
He'll have no money at all.

BOSIE sits back down.

BOSIE

Oh, so you're blaming me, too, now are you!

ROSS

I'm not blaming anyone, Bosie. You're not the only person on
this earth Oscar cares about.

BOSIE

You've always hated me Robbie! Because Oscar *loved* and still
loves me when you were never more than one of his boys! I'm
suffering just as much as he is, you know!

ROSS doubts this very much, but doesn't say so.

BOSIE*(cont.)*

My life's ruined, too. I'm much younger than he is. I've hardly
had any life, and it's ruined already. When Oscar gets out, we'll
live together properly. We'll take a villa somewhere near here:
Posillipo or Ischia or Capri. I'll take care of him – I'll give him
everything he wants. I love him, Robbie.

This is obvious fantasy and ROSS's opinion of it shows on his face.

BOSIE*(cont.)*
Oscar's mine! And I'm going to have him!

He jumps up and marches off. ROSS does not attempt to follow.

We hear OSCAR reading The Selfish Giant *over.*

OSCAR(O/S)
Years went over, and the giant grew very old and very feeble.

97

INTERIOR

Reading Gaol

1896. DAY

OSCAR is alone in his comfortless cell. He is a wreck of what he was. His chamber pot is overflowing. He is weeping. Story continues over.

OSCAR(O/S)
He couldn't play about any more, so he sat in a huge armchair...

98

EXTERIOR

Reading Gaol

TREADMILL. 1896. DAY

The PRISONERS are on the treadmill. Story continues.

OSCAR(O/S)

...and watched the children at their games,
and admired his garden.

99

INTERIOR

Reading Gaol

1896. DAY

In OSCAR's cell we see OSCAR collapse.

OSCAR(O/S)

'I have many beautiful flowers', he said,
'but the children are the most beautiful flowers of all.'

100

SCENE INSERT

Tite Street

WINDOW

FLASH CUT: of CYRIL and VYVYAN at the window.

101

INTERIOR

Reading Gaol

PRIVATE INTERVIEW ROOM. 1896. DAY

CONSTANCE has come to visit OSCAR. She is very shocked by his condition.

CONSTANCE
I'm afraid Cyril has got some idea of why you're here. I'm sending them to school in Germany. I can't manage them on my own.

OSCAR
Your back isn't better, then?

CONSTANCE
No. Not really. I may have to have an operation.

OSCAR takes another moment. But even now, though he is sorry, he can't deny his own nature.

OSCAR *(cont.)*
What I've done to you, and the boys – I can't – I shall never forgive myself.

(he looks to her for help)

OSCAR *(cont.)*

If we could choose our natures. If we could only choose. But it's no use. Whatever our natures are, we must fulfil them. Or our lives – my life would have been filled with dishonesty … even more dishonesty than there actually was.

(he looks up again)

I've always loved you, Constance. You must believe me.

CONSTANCE can only speak the truth now.

CONSTANCE

I don't see how you can have done. Not truly. Not if, all the time –

OSCAR

I didn't know. Know thyself, I used to say. I didn't know myself. I didn't know.

She looks him in the eyes.

OSCAR *(cont.)*

I suppose you want a divorce? You have every reason.

CONSTANCE

I've been thinking. When you do come out, when they let you out, you can go to Switzerland or Italy, write another play, get yourself back –

He shakes his head.

CONSTANCE *(cont.)*

You can. You're so clever, you can –

He says nothing. Her heart melts.

CONSTANCE

Oscar, I don't want a divorce.

OSCAR

Will you ever let me see the children again?

CONSTANCE

Of course.

He is full of joy at the thought.

CONSTANCE*(cont.)*

But there must be one condition, Oscar. You must never see Bosie again.

He looks at her through tear-filled eyes.

OSCAR

If I saw Bosie now, I'd kill him.

She is very cheered to hear this.

CONSTANCE

The children love you, Oscar.

She takes his hand.

CONSTANCE*(cont.)*

They'll always love you. Did anyone tell you? They've been performing *Salome* in Paris.

102

INTERIOR

Reading Gaol

CELL. 1897. DAY

OSCAR has been given paper, and is allowed to write.

OSCAR(v/o)

The giant hastened across the grass, and came near to the child. And when he came quite close his face grew red with anger, and he said: 'Who hath dared to wound thee?' For on the palms of the child's hands were the prints of two nails, and the prints of two nails were on his little feet.

A WARDER comes in. OSCAR bundles the pieces of paper together and gives them to him.

The WARDER goes. OSCAR goes to his barred window and gazes at the small square of sky.

> OSCAR (V/O)
> 'Who hath dared to wound thee?' cried the giant;
> 'tell me that I may take my big sword and slay him.'
> 'Nay!' answered the child, 'but these are the
> wounds of love.'

103

EXTERIOR

Goring House

1893. DAY

A fleeting image of CONSTANCE, waving.

104

INTERIOR

London Hotel

SITTING-ROOM. 1897. DAY

ROSS is with ADA in a private booth in a quiet corner of the sitting-room, having tea. ROSS is very dejected.

> ROSS
> Bosie thinks I'm jealous.

She just touches his arm.

ADA

I think it will come as a shock to Bosie to realize that even he is relatively unimportant in the scheme of things. But no doubt Bosie will be remembered as long as Oscar, unfortunately.

ROSS

I sometimes wonder, if I hadn't – pushed him – into –

ADA

Don't. Oscar was very lucky to meet you, Robbie. Think who else it might have been.

He is very grateful.

ADA *(cont.)*

Must you go abroad again at once?

ROSS

I shouldn't be here now.

ADA

But – has he got anywhere to go when he's released?

ROSS

It'll have to be in France. I'm going to see what I can arrange.

ADA

But here – when he leaves prison?

105

EXTERIOR

Pentonville Prison

1897. DAY

OSCAR is emerging from prison, carrying a suitcase and a large manila envelope. He has lost a lot of weight. ADA, wearing a smart hat, waits for him with a cab.

OSCAR
Goodbye, Mr Harris. Goodbye, Mr Smith. Thank you.
                     ADA
Oscar.

                    OSCAR
My dear Sphinx, how marvellous of you to know what hat to
wear at seven in the morning to meet a friend who has been
away!

She kisses him warmly. The CABMAN wants to take the envelope and put it with the case.
                 OSCAR *(cont.)*
No – I'll keep this.
                     ADA
What is it?

                    OSCAR
It's a letter to Bosie, telling him how I love him but can never
see him again. I'm going to ask Robbie to have it copied before
I send it. I rather fear Bosie might throw it on the fire.

He gets in the cab with ADA.
                 OSCAR *(cont.)*
I call it *De Profundis*. It comes from the very depths.

106

EXTERIOR

Berneval Beach

1897. EVENING

*A storm is crashing waves down on the beach. OSCAR, wrapped in a cloak, is walking along
the deserted front, ROSS following at a distance. We hear OSCAR reciting his last poem
over.*

OSCAR (O/S)
I know not whether Laws be right,
  Or whether Laws be wrong;
All that we know who lie in gaol
  Is that the wall is strong;
And that each day is like a year,
  A year whose days are long.

107

EXTERIOR

Italian Cemetery

DAY

OSCAR is walking towards a grave. He kneels down before it.

He lays a posy of flowers on the grave and we see it is that of CONSTANCE. ROSS stays at a tactful distance.

OSCAR (O/S)
Yet each man kills the thing he loves,
  By each let this be heard,
Some do it with a bitter look,
  Some with a flattering word.
The coward does it with a kiss,
  The brave man with a sword!

Some kill their love when they are young,
  And some when they are old;
Some strangle with the hands of Lust,
  Some with the hands of Gold:
The kindest use a knife, because
  The dead so soon grow cold.

108

French Café

1898. DAY

OSCAR is sitting with ROSS.

> ROSS
>
> I'm sure we can find an hotel near here. Somewhere where you can work.

Silence.

> OSCAR
>
> I've decided to see him again, Robbie.

> ROSS
>
> Yes. I thought you might.

> OSCAR
>
> I have nothing left. I've lost my wife, I've lost my children — they won't allow me to see them now. No one will ever read my plays or books again.

> ROSS
>
> Yes they will!

> OSCAR
>
> Bosie loves me more than he loves anyone else. As much as he can love. And allow himself to be loved.

> ROSS
>
> I think we need some more wine. I find that alcohol, taken in sufficient quantities . . .

> OSCAR
>
> . . . Can bring about all the effects of drunkenness.

109

Colonaded Piazza

1898. DAY

BOSIE is arriving in a carriage with mounds of luggage. He looks as young and beautiful as ever. PORTERS rush out of the small hotel to attend him. OSCAR is in the shadows of the pillars, watching.

> OSCAR (o/s)
> Life cheats us with shadows. We ask it for pleasure. It gives it to us, with bitterness and disappointment in its train. And we find ourselves looking with dull heart of stone at the tress of gold-flecked hair that we had once so wildly worshipped and so madly kissed.

BOSIE turns and sees OSCAR. He grins.

> BOSIE
> Oscar!

OSCAR's look is very equivocal. He steps out of the shadows and raises his hat. He starts to move slowly, almost unwillingly, towards the waiting BOSIE.

> OSCAR (o/s)
> In this world there are only two tragedies. One is not getting what one wants. The other is getting it.

He moves slowly towards his doom.

FADE TO BLACK.

LIFE AFTER DEATH

JULIAN MITCHELL

ONCE upon a time in Cochin, on the Coast of Coromandel, a film location manager was asked to find as many elephants as he could as soon as possible for a scene in *Gandhi*. Now most elephants in Kerala belong to temples, where they stand all day in an outer courtyard, tapping tourists on the head with their trunks in return for a few rupees. It's a dull, if sacred, life, and the priests were reluctant to part with their revenue-generating beasts without generous donations to Shiva and Laxshmi. Films being films – everything is always urgent in the cinema – the gods were at once offered the most generous terms, and soon the roads of South India were jammed with elephants plodding their way to the location. They took their time; elephants can only plod about fifty miles a day. But at last they were all assembled, clothed in their most splendid vestments, their necks hung with garlands, and their noble heads painted red and yellow. Their mahouts sat proudly on top of them in elaborate howdahs. With loud trumpeting the filming got under way.

PREVIOUS PAGE The scriptwriter (Julian Mitchell) joins the jury to make sure they deliver the right verdict. Which was, of course, the wrong one.

OPPOSITE Noel Cowell of the props department sets the scene as the director Brian Gilbert prepares Constance (Jennifer Ehle) for the bad news that she'll have to leave the country.

Next day the mahouts collected their pay, and the elephants started the long plod back to their mundane religious life. The whole business took hundreds of men and elephants about a week. And not a single frame appeared in the final film.

I'm afraid this story must seem preposterous to most people outside the film industry, a fantastic waste of time and money. But no one in the industry will raise an eyebrow. Films are made in the cutting room, not on location, and there's always a very high percentage of waste material. But – why?

A film is made from a 'shooting script', and ideally this should contain everything that will appear on the screen, and nothing more. It should be a genuine blueprint for the finished film. And producer, director and writer go through it time and time again to try to make it just that. No one, after all, actually wants to waste money on scenes that aren't going to be used. But once shooting begins the script is simply the starting point for director, cast and crew, and however carefully you've prepared, you don't know what you've got till you've got it. You don't even know how long your film is going to be – cinema is not TV, with an exact time-slot to fill. Experts can and do spend days trying to estimate the length – but in the end a film is as long as it needs to be, and that's all you can say.

The shooting script has numbered scenes – Wilde originally had 122. The director and lighting cameraman cover each scene with different shots from different angles. Each shot is repeated till everyone's satisfied. This can be after one take or twenty. Technical things are always going wrong, and it often needs several goes before an actor gives his or her best performance. Not all takes are printed, but thousands are, and every evening, after the day's shoot, the director and editor (with others professionally concerned) watch the previous day's rushes, the director indicating which takes he thinks best. The editor steadily assembles these, and when filming is over produces an editor's cut, using his own skill and judgement to create the first coherent version of the finished film. As everything is kept at this stage, the editor's cut is always much too long, and it's seen only by the director and producer. But it's the basis from which the director and editor now work, whittling away at it for months, trying different takes, cutting here, cutting there, dispensing with what now seems irrelevant, and improving performances by judicious editing. They will make several different full-length versions before the final director's cut. It is here, in the dark of the editing suite, that a director exercises as much, if not more, personal artistic judgement as he has used under the

lights of the set. He shows his individual character as a director through the instinct by which he makes his choices. (Different directors would make very different films from the same material.) If instinct tells him to cut a scene which has seemed essential to everyone concerned since the very start of the project, then out the scene goes, however many elephants plodded however many miles to make it.

The producer may weep at this and wring his hands, wishing they were around the director's neck, but unless he wants a major row – directors may think they're gods, but they can be fired – he has to let the director decide what's going to be in his cut and what's not. At this stage no one else has any say. Between the last day of shooting and the director's cut, whole scenes and characters may have disappeared, while others have been severely pruned, or moved from one place to another in the story. Why can't anyone have foreseen this? Because in the process of film-making there are simply too many variables.

First, there is the quality of the performances. A film actor can convey great emotion by the quiver of

Oscar and Robbie Ross about to rediscover the effects of alcohol under the watchful eyes of the camera crew and ears of Simon Firsht, boom operator.

an eyelid; things which are spelt out in dialogue can be conveyed in a single covert glance. So lines which may have been necessary for the actor to understand how to give that look become redundant in the film. Also the film director works very intimately with his actors. He is never more than a few feet from them during shooting; he can get them to try things neither he nor they have thought of till that take. Then scenes play longer or shorter than imagined, and have greater or less impact; some which were supposed to advance the action turn out to hold it up; particular performers don't bring the expected qualities to their roles; others bring much more; explanatory scenes suddenly become unnecessary; emotional repetitions are discovered where none were suspected; editorializing is revealed and ruthlessly suppressed. There is, too, the visual impact of certain locations in certain weathers, the effect of the designer's work, the effect of the camera work. Thus what the director has to play with in the cutting room is often very different from what was written on the page. It is because a film changes its nature in this way during its making that there is liable to be between ten and twenty per cent wastage. It may seem an astonishingly high amount, but for all the technical sophistication of the industry and its army

Stephen Fry cools down in the
Cadogan Hotel with Michael Sheen
and Brian Gilbert warns them of
Oscar's approaching arrest.

of specialists, films are essentially dependent on the very varied talents of many individuals, with all the risks that implies. The experienced producer knows this and grits his teeth. The reason he's bald is that he's torn out his hair trying to reduce the variables to sensible proportions; and failed.

Editing is a highly enjoyable part of film-making and there is powerful temptation to keep trying new combinations of shots and takes for ever. But after what seems to everyone else an intolerable delay, the director shows his cut, very much shorter than the editor's and getting close to the final film. This cut is very difficult to judge, as it is still without its proper music, and the print has not been graded. It is shown only to the few people most directly concerned, who then deluge the director with their comments and suggestions. He listens to these, with or without a smile, considers and digests, then goes back with the editor to work for more weeks on the final cut. (In the case of *Wilde*, the director's cut was almost a quarter of an hour longer than the finished film.) Then comes the 'looping' - the revoicing of scenes where the sound is unsatisfactory: you can add new lines here, if you need, as voice-overs, or fill in the background chat of crowd scenes. A soundtrack is a combination of many, many separate tracks, and its impact is often much greater than the viewer, absorbed in visual images, realizes. The final soundtrack, including the music, takes several weeks to mix. And there at last is the film you see in the cinema. The script of this final version, such as is published here, bears a close family resemblance to the shooting script with which filming started, but it's not the same thing at all. Just as the shooting script has come a long way from its own first draft.

Biographical films have special problems, some technical, some moral. No one can really know what it's like to be even someone very close; how much harder to know what a stranger was like a hundred years ago. Then you have only two hours or so to tell your story, which means making many compromises with historical truth – always supposing you're sure what that is. You collapse time, so events that really took place years apart follow one on top of the other, and you fiddle the sequence to make it more dramatic. You merge two or three minor characters into one for convenience (and to make a better part so you can get a better actor). You invent people to put across points of view you think you need, but which no one at the time was obliging enough to express. Where you know what people actually said, you edit it down and modernize it to your needs. But though you are making a dramatic

Last day of shooting for Jennifer Ehle. Brian
Gilbert awards her a bottle of champagne for
beauty and constancy.

entertainment, not giving a history lesson, you still want to remain 'true' in some sense to your subject. You aim to tell not 'the' truth (as though anyone ever could), but at least 'a' truth - to convey what you feel is the essence of your story. And to do that, you use your imagination.

One of the problems of writing about Oscar Wilde - quite apart from having to write convincing dialogue for one of the wittiest men in British history - is that so many people have let their imaginations roam round the subject so luridly already. But I had the great advantage or starting from Richard Ellmann's magisterial biography. Not that I was confined to Ellmann's interpretation - indeed, I sometimes disagreed with him profoundly. But he was a wonderful guide through the dense and sometimes fantastic forest of Wildeana. Some of the most irresponsible inventions were those of Lord Alfred Douglas, the young Bosie with whom Wilde fell so catastrophically in love. Bosie wrote several versions of their story, and started furious libel actions against anyone who dared to question them. He was particularly bitter towards Robert Ross, Wilde's first male lover, for whom Bosie seems to have felt the greatest jealousy. I find Ross a most attractive character, admirably loyal to Wilde in life and death, whereas Bosie was neither, and I had to be careful not to be prejudiced in Ross's favour while describing their rivalry. Bosie's antagonism was fierce even before Wilde died, and he went completely out of control when Ross published an abridged version of *De Profundis* in 1905. This was Wilde's own version of his affair with Bosie, written in Reading Gaol. Though it's in the form of a letter to Bosie, Wilde gave Ross a copy, knowing that Bosie would in all likelihood destroy it. Bosie, who comes out of it badly, was even angrier when Ross, as part of his continuing campaign to restore Wilde's reputation, got Arthur Ransome to write the first biography in 1912. Bosie brought a libel action, during which Ross had the whole of *De Profundis* read out in court. Bosie walked out rather than listen in public to Wilde's accusations. From then on he harried Ross at every turn – even, as some people think, to death. Ross died in 1918, shortly after the most spectacular of Bosie's attacks.

This came during the trial for libel of a crazed Tory MP called Pemberton Billing who claimed, among other insanities, that the reason Britain wasn't winning the First World War was that the German High Command had a list of 40,000 homosexuals in the highest reaches of British social and political life and was blackmailing them to hinder the British war effort. (They included Mrs Asquith, wife of the last

Prime Minister, and the judge trying the case.) Bosie came to give evidence on Billing's behalf and, taking advantage of the freedom of the court to say anything he liked, announced that there was a conspiracy to prevent Ross from being prosecuted for sodomy, and that Oscar Wilde was the greatest force for evil of the last 350 years. Twenty-three years after Oscar's trials he was in court again, accused of being responsible for the disasters of the Western Front. This was life after death indeed.

Screenplays are always collaborations - mainly between writer and director, but with the producer keeping a close eye. In the case of *Wilde* I didn't start to write till I'd spent many hours in discussion with Brian Gilbert, and Marc and Peter Samuelson had commented in detail on all the drafts. We were anxious that Wilde should be seen not simply as a figure from the past, but as someone whose life and work has continued to be painfully relevant to British society for the last hundred years. The Pemberton Billing case seemed a wonderful example of how he managed to get under some people's skin long after they thought they'd got him safely dead and buried. So we thought we might start the story there.

As part of the preparation before writing, what writers grandly call 'research', I felt I must go to Paris to visit Wilde's left bank haunts, and of course

his grave. He is buried in Père Lachaise cemetery where a splendid sphinx, designed by Jacob Epstein, was erected over the grave - at Ross's instigation. The sphinx has - or should have - a very manly member, but admirers keep stealing it. As you walk along the paths past the many elaborate tombs and famous names - Proust is here, and Edith Piaf - you quickly realize that Père Lachaise is not just a graveyard, it is a site of pilgrimage, notably for devotees of Jim Morrison, whose name is scrawled and painted everywhere. There isn't any graffiti celebrating Oscar, I'm glad to say, but his tomb too is a shrine. There were already fresh flowers when I arrived on a cold wet autumn day, and a young man and young woman from New Zealand were opening a bottle of champagne. They poured a libation, then toasted his memory. More people kept arriving from all over the world to pay their homage, and I realized for the first time what an enormously popular and potent figure Oscar still is, nearly a hundred years after his death. Who else from his period, in the English-speaking world, is still loved and remembered? Perhaps only Winston Churchill.

Marc Samuelson, producer, requesting his Harley Street surgeon to graft a second mobile phone to his other ear. The scene is Magdalen College, Oxford.

As soon as I saw this scene – 'witnessed' is perhaps the appropriate word – I felt our film should start there, at Père Lachaise, with pilgrims gay and straight, men and women, young and old, celebrating Oscar's achievement at his tomb. This could be cross-cut with the Pemberton Billing trial and scenes from the slaughter on the Western Front – showing how Oscar was a living presence throughout the century, always on trial in the minds of certain people, but triumphant over his enemies. At the end I wanted the pilgrims to turn and see the great writer strolling towards them, wearing one of his broad black hats and carrying a cane. He would smile as he passed through them, and vanish into the future, where he would go on being celebrated long after they were gone.

But – this was more about Oscar and his legend than the classical tragedy of the love affair with Bosie Douglas from which the legend arose. So we abandoned Père Lachaise and Pemberton Billing, without abandoning the idea of Oscar as a living presence. We decided instead to begin with newsreel of the dedication of the window to Oscar in Poets' Corner in Westminster Abbey. The fact that someone sentenced to two years' hard labour could end up in the Abbey a hundred years later, utterly reversing society's original judgement, seemed to show just

Martin Fuhrer, director of photography, checks the bloom on the cheek of Jack Knight (Cyril Wilde) as he prepares for a gallop on his rocking-horse.

how much Oscar still haunts the British conscience. But this again proved a distraction from the real story, which is how a married man and devoted father fell fatally in love with a young man. Constance Wilde and the children were as much victims of the tragedy as Oscar himself. Bosie was a victim, too, living on till 1945, never able to face or escape the only truly important relationship of his life. Westminster Abbey was a distraction. The story needed no introduction, no top and tailing, no brackets.

So we started again, this time with *Patience*, the Gilbert and Sullivan operetta which, though the satire is quite mild and unfocussed, was widely thought to be a send-up of the young Wilde. Brian is very fond of Gilbert and Sullivan, whereas I am almost totally allergic. But it was to advertize *Patience* that Oscar went to America – where of course he told the customs officers that he had 'nothing to declare but his genius', a line which at that time we felt we couldn't possibly leave out. (It's gone!) But *Patience* required too much time and explanation. It wasn't the meat of the story, it was hardly more than the soup course, and we know what Oscar thought about soup. So we began with Oscar's arrival in New York. By this time, I had been reading and writing about Oscar for more than six months and had done some five different drafts. The fifth became the basis on which Marc and Peter Samuelson set out to raise money to make the film.

When we came back to it, almost six months later, we saw the story much clearer for our absence and made radical changes. The truth about homosexual love can be told without embarrassment or shame now, we don't have to hide behind the euphemisms and innuendo of earlier film-makers, and if we had a message, it was simply that love is love wherever you find it, and whoever with. We didn't need introductions or explanations. We simply had to show how a bisexual genius came to discover his homosexual side, and where that led him. We could start in Leadville, Colorado, with Oscar going down a silver mine to talk to the miners about Cellini. The scene had been there all along, but now it suddenly seemed emblematic, with Oscar plunging from the sunshine of the surface to the depths of the mine. We also very drastically shortened the end. The last two years of Oscar's life, after he comes out of prison, are a terrible story of decline which would make a harrowing movie on their own. But our focus was now on the love story, and that ends, really, when Oscar breaks his promise never to see Bosie again, and returns to him, knowing it will never work. The true historical ending was slow, complicated, messy and lacked drama – so we have tidied it up, and will no doubt be criticized for doing so. But though things did not literally happen as we've shown them, we believe the essence of the doomed relationship is there. We have made a film.

Oscar and Bosie stroll beside the river at Magdalen College, Oxford, with Darren Quinn, Mike Miller and Sam Garwood of the camera crew toiling in their wake.

THE CAST

Oscar Wilde . . . . Stephen Fry

Lord Alfred Douglas . . . . Jude Law

Lady 'Speranza' Wilde . . . . Vanessa Redgrave

Constance Wilde . . . . Jennifer Ehle

Lady Queensberry . . . . Gemma Jones

Lady Mount-Temple . . . . Judy Parfitt

Robert Ross . . . . Michael Sheen

Ada Leverson . . . . Zoë Wanamaker

The Marquess of Queensberry . . . . Tom Wilkinson

John Gray . . . . Ioan Gruffudd

Charles Gill . . . . Peter Barkworth

C. O. Humphreys . . . . Robert Lang

Judge . . . . Philip Locke

Edward Carson . . . . David Westhead

Cyril Wilde . . . . Jack Knight

Cyril Wilde, aged 4 . . . . Jackson Leach

Vyvyan Wilde . . . . Laurence Owen

Alfred Wood . . . . Benedict Sandiford

Charles Parker . . . . Mark Letheren

Alfred Taylor . . . . Michael Fitzgerald

Rentboy . . . . Orlando Bloom

Mine Owner . . . . Bob Sessions

George Alexander . . . . Robin Kermode

Hotel Manager . . . . James Vaughan

THE LOCATIONS

CAFÉ ROYAL, REGENT STREET, LONDON W1

Established in 1865, the Café Royal has long been associated with London's literati. Many famous faces have dined there. In the film, during a lunch with Lord Alfred Douglas (Bosie), Oscar meets the Marquess of Queensberry for the first time.

2 SOUTH AUDLEY STREET, LONDON W1

This beautiful listed building off Park Lane was used extensively during filming. While the interior doubled for Wilde's home in Tite Street, the exterior was a perfect substitute for the Cadogan Hotel. Christmas at the Wildes' was filmed in the ground floor front room and Oscar's study was created in another panelled room. Rubber cobbles were laid to cover the modern tarmac and horse-drawn carriages filled South Audley Street for most of the day.

26 TREDEGAR SQUARE, LONDON EC3

This East London location was used as Speranza's drawing room where we first see Oscar and Constance together. There was little space for much manoeuvring but the crew had 'fun' creating a busy 'at home' with supporting artists delicately weaving their way around a tiny room.

HOUGHTON LODGE, NEAR STOCKBRIDGE, HAMPSHIRE

The Wilde family often visited their summer house in Goring-on-Thames to escape London life. Houghton Lodge at Houghton, near Stockbridge, was the perfect location. By a winding river with luxurious lawns and topiary gardens, the house looks out across miles of Hampshire fields. The crew filmed Oscar's children fishing with their father during their stay in 1893 here, as well as Bosie and friends relaxing on the lawn later the same year. The study in which Wilde and Bosie have their first fight was a circular room with a unique domed ceiling. The sound department, with the help of a highly skilled construction unit, had to build a false ceiling to control the sound as the dimensions naturally created the effect of a whispering gallery.

LUTON HOO, BEDFORDSHIRE

This grand Bedfordshire mansion set in acres of woodland and rolling pastures has been a backdrop for many filmmakers over the years. The original living room was converted by the *Wilde* art department into a flamboyant London hotel foyer, while the upstairs rooms were set-dressed to represent the beautiful hotel suites occupied by Wilde during the height of his popularity. A small servants' quarters at the top of the house was also transformed into Taylor's flat where Oscar, along with Bosie, 'feasted with panthers'.

MAGDALEN COLLEGE, OXFORD
Wilde was at Magdalen College during his student days. The College was extremely helpful in allowing us access to the grounds and residences to obtain effective architectural accuracy. The Oscar/Bosie stroll scene was shot on the banks of the Cherwell River by Addison Walk in the College grounds. The singing scene and Bosie's bedroom scene took place in the Master's beautiful residence.

DURDLE DOOR, NEAR SWANAGE, DORSET
The sheer cliffs of this area of the Dorset coastline became a dramatic backdrop for Constance's and the boys' visit to Babbacombe Beach. Durdle means 'pierced' or 'through' and the dramatic limestone erosion has left a giant hole or 'door' in the peninsula. Four-wheel-drive off-road vehicles had to be used to shuttle equipment to this remote location which then had to be carried by hand down over a hundred steps to the beach. With the help of local residents, the same process had to be reversed at the end of the day's shooting, making this an exhausting but worthwhile location.

JAMAICA WINE HOUSE, LONDON EC3

This old public house was established in 1869, although the owners claim that it had been recognized as a meeting house for some two hundred years. The bar scene with Ross and Gray was shot here. The history of the Jamaica itself is extensive. The alley in which the bar is situated was destroyed in the Great Fire of 1666 and records after were vague as to its reinstatement. A report dating back to 1755 recorded that William Hickey was directed to the Jamaica to acquire a passage to the West Indies.

KNEBWORTH HOUSE, HERTFORDSHIRE

This famous house, used on several occasions by the film industry for its gothic exterior and grand rooms, was used by the *Wilde* crew as Lady Queensberry's residence. The state drawing-room, entrance hall and banqueting hall were all featured. The house has been under the ownership of the Lytton family since 1492, although the gothic trimmings were added during the middle of the nineteenth century. The renowned novelist Edward Bulwer Lytton often entertained Charles Dickens there. While filming, the crew were shown an original copy of one of Wilde's publications by Lord Cobbold. It had been signed and dedicated by Oscar to the Lytton Family.

OXFORD PRISON

Although Reading Gaol still stands, it is now a remand centre for young offenders and is architecturally quite removed from its original appearance during Wilde's term there. Instead, the crew located themselves at the recently closed Oxford Prison where they reconstructed Oscar's cell and the gaol's prison yard. As a form of humiliation (aside from the hell of the treadmill) the inmates were forced to wear hoods to cover their faces when exercising in the yard.

SWANAGE PIER

Despite attracting over three hundred spectators to see naked male bathers dive off the end of Swanage Pier, the crew were able to film the Wilde family enjoying a seaside outing to Worthing, and Bosie's promenade along the ornate Victorian structure. Special safety divers were called in to keep an eye on the swimmers, but they needed no persuasion to leap from the pier in front of a cheering crowd.

FINCA EL SABINAR, ALICANTE/GRANADA, SPAIN

This vast landscape in Spain was utilized for the opening scene set in Leadville, Colorado. Spanish horsemen and supporting artists re-enacted with great enthusiasm the arrival of Wilde at the Matchless Mines in 1882. As well as America, Spain was used for the Italian cemetery where Wilde visits his wife's grave. Stephen Fry, Michael Sheen and the crew filmed at dawn in a small cemetery near the Alhambra, Granada, emphasizing the serenity of this powerful scene. The old streets of Granada also doubled for a small French town where Oscar and Ross have lunch. The art department altered the fronts of the surrounding houses to adopt a French feel, while the costume department meticulously dressed the Spanish supporting artists in appropriate costume.

IAN THOMSON

$\mathcal{B}$IOGRAPHIES

JULIAN MITCHELL was educated at Winchester and Oxford and has been a freelance writer since 1962. A prizewinning novelist and playwright, he has written copiously for television since 1966, beginning with an adaptation of his own play, *A Heritage and Its History* and continuing with Somerset Maugham's *The Alien Corn*. Among his many original plays are: 'Shadow in the Sun' (Emmy, 1971) in the series *Elizabeth R*, *A Question of Degree*, *Rust*, the series *Jennie*, *Lady Randolph Churchill*, *Abide With Me* (International Critics' Prize, Monte Carlo, and US Humanities Award, 1977), *The Mysterious Stranger* (Golden Eagle, 1983), nine episodes of *Inspector Morse* (many awards and prizes) and *Survival of the Fittest*. He has also adapted many books for television, including *The Weather in The Streets*, *Staying On* and *The Good Soldier*. For the cinema, he has written *Arabesque* (Stanley Donen, 1965), *Another Country* (Marek Kanievska, 1984), based on his own award-winning stage play, *Vincent and Theo* (Robert Altman, 1990) and *August* (Anthony Hopkins, 1995).

STEPHEN FRY – actor, comedian, novelist, journalist, screenwriter – is a hugely versatile writer and performer, whose wit and talent were first recognized at Cambridge University, where he acted in more than thirty plays and won Edinburgh Festival Fringe awards for his writing contributions. Whilst at Cambridge, he also wrote and performed with the Footlights, the celebrated revue company, and his comedy skills were soon enlisted by the BBC, where he wrote and performed in such classic series as *Not the Nine O'Clock News*, *The Young Ones*, *Blackadder* and *A Bit of Fry and Laurie*. He has played the imperturbable Jeeves opposite his friend and writing partner Hugh Laurie's Bertie in four series of Granada's *Jeeves and Wooster* and has acted in a variety of films, including *The Good Father*, *A Handful of Dust*, *A Fish Called Wanda*, *Peter's Friends*, *I.Q.*, *Cold Comfort Farm*, *The Steal* and *The Wind in the Willows*. His latest novel, *Making History*, is published by Hutchinson.

BRIAN GILBERT, the director, began his career in films as an actor, before spending three years at the National Film and Television School, where his graduation film, *The Devotee*, came to the attention of David Puttnam, who commissioned him to write and direct *Sharma and Beyond* for Channel Four's *First Love* series. In 1984, he directed his first theatrical feature, *The Frog Prince*, also for Puttnam, and this was followed by two successful American studio features, *Vice Versa*, starring Judge Reinhold and *Not Without My Daughter*, starring Sally Field and Alfred Molina, which he also wrote. In 1994, he returned to the UK to direct the award-winning *Tom and Viv*, starring Willem Dafoe as T. S. Eliot, Miranda Richardson as his wife Vivienne Haigh-Wood and Rosemary Harris as her mother Rose, for producers Marc and Peter Samuelson. *Tom and Viv* received two Oscar nominations, two BAFTA nominations, a Golden Globe nomination and won for Best Actress at the National Board of Review.

ISBN 0-7871-1411-1

DOVE BOOKS
8955 Beverly Boulevard
Los Angeles, CA 90048

Distributed by Penguin USA

Photograph of Oscar Wilde on page 6: reproduced by
kind permission of Corbis–Bettmann
Stills photography by Liam Daniel
DESIGNED BY THE BRIDGEWATER BOOK COMPANY LTD
Project editor: Natasha Martyn-Johns

First printing: August 1997

10 9 8 7 6 5 4 3 2 1

Color reproduction in Italy by Newsele, Litho Spa, Milan
Printed in Italy by Printers, Trento
Bound in Italy by L.E.G.O., Vicenza